Gentleman In the Outdoors

Gentleman
IN THE Outdoors

A PORTRAIT OF
MAX C. FLEISCHMANN

SESSIONS S. WHEELER

Foreword by
Governor Mike O'Callaghan

University of Nevada Press
Reno, 1985

Publication of this book has been supported by a generous gift from Nabisco Brands, Inc., Parsippany, New Jersey.

Library of Congress Cataloging in Publication Data

Wheeler, Sessions S.
  Gentleman in the outdoors.

  Includes index.
  1. Fleischmann, Max C. (Max Charles), 1877–1951.
2. Hunting. 3. Fishing 4. Outdoor life. 5. Naturalists—United States—Biography. 6. Philanthropists—
United States—Biography. I. Title.
QH31.F59W47   1985   338.7'664'68   [B]   85–8753
ISBN 0–87417–098–2

University of Nevada Press, Reno, Nevada 89557 USA
© University of Nevada Press 1985. All rights reserved
Design by Dave Comstock
Printed in the United States of America

I like a book to have a dedication, and at breakfast of the day I hoped to complete the manuscript, I wondered what the Major would have wished me to write. And then the thought came that he would have said, "Buck, dedicate it to my wife, Sarah, who walked many back-country trails with me and, above all else, was my very best friend."

Books by Sessions S. Wheeler

Paiute

The Desert Lake
The Story of Nevada's Pyramid Lake

The Nevada Desert

Nevada's Black Rock Desert

Gentleman in the Outdoors
A Portrait of Max C. Fleischmann

Contents

Foreword

Major Max C. Fleischmann left an immeasurable impact on Nevada and Nevadans. No other person has contributed more to the Silver State and its residents.

During the eight years this writer served as governor of Nevada, the Fleischmann Foundation was synonymous with dollars for worthy educational, health, and environmental projects designed for the people of our state.

I leave it to author Sessions "Buck" Wheeler to relate the astounding number of contributions the Max C. Fleischmann Foundation made to better the quality of life for several generations of Nevadans.

Becoming acquainted with Major Fleischmann through Wheeler's eyes is both a revelation and a pleasure. The total man—soldier, hunter, fisherman, friend, explorer, husband, and businessman—becomes real. Wheeler's Fleischmann is a man I wish I had known during the years he lived in the state of Nevada.

Men get to know each other better when fishing a trout stream than they do sitting in a board room. There is no rank among fishermen and hunters. Everybody takes his turn breaking trail and cooking over the campfire in the outdoors. The trips the author took with Max Fleischmann reveal a man of spirit, kindliness, and wisdom. As a reader it made me wish I had been with the Major and Wheeler on at least one outing.

There were others during this period who gave their time and talents to the betterment of the state, including my friend Judge Clark J. Guild. The author includes them in this memorable book about one of Nevada's greatest benefactors, Major Max C. Fleischmann.

Mike O'Callaghan
Governor of Nevada, 1971–78

Acknowledgments

I am very grateful to the following people and organizations who provided aid in obtaining information or whose cooperation in some way helped this book:

Mr. and Mrs. Julius Bergen; Mr. Robert Laxalt; Mrs. Susan Conway and other personnel of the Getchell Library at the University of Nevada, Reno, including Mr. Tim Gorelangton of the Special Collections department and the staff of the Oral History Project and Interlibrary Loan departments; Mr. James R. Hunt, Librarian of the Public Library of Cincinnati and Hamilton County, Ohio; the Military Archives Division of the National Archives, Washington, D.C.; Mr. Jimmy Robinson, Minneapolis, Minnesota; Ducks Unlimited, Inc., Long Grove, Illinois; Mr. Dennis M. Power, Director of the Santa Barbara Museum of Natural History; Mr. Robert Nylen and Mrs. Judy Hendrix of the Nevada State Museum; Ms. Lennan Guild; Mr. Clark J. Guild, Jr.; Mr. Morley W. Griswold; Mr. David Hurst Thomas of the American Museum of Natural History, New York, N.Y.; the University of Utah Libraries; Ms. Caroline J. Hadley, *Nevada* magazine; Mr. Charles Fleischmann, Cincinnati, Ohio; Mr. Christian Holmes, Washington, D.C.; Mrs. Dielle Fleischmann Seignious, Plains, Virginia; Mrs. Janet E. Baldwin, Librarian, The Explorers Club, New York, N.Y.; Mrs. Clara Robison; Mr. Dave Rice, Nevada State Department of Wildlife; Mr. Harold Curran; Mr. Ron Evenson and the staff of the photography laboratory, Office of Communications and Broadcasting, University of Nevada, Reno; Mr. Joseph T. McDonnell; Nevada State Library; Mr. Walter G. Dunnington, Jr.; Francis Breen; and Clayton Phillips.

I also wish to express gratitude to the book's capable and pleasant editor, Mrs. Cameron Sutherland, and to Director John F. Stetter, Editor-in-Chief Nick Cady, and other personnel of the University of Nevada Press.

Author's Note

Most of this book is a story of one man's love for the outdoors. It is not a comprehensive biography.

It may be of particular interest to sportsmen, but I hope it also will be enjoyable reading for others who may wish to become better acquainted with a remarkable man whose life was filled with adventure and whose money has in some way, large or small, benefited untold millions of Americans.

His name was known throughout much of this country and in other parts of the world. But I am certain that he received more satisfaction from his ability as a naturalist than he did from the prestige his wealth provided.

He could be tough, but he was never arrogant or pompous. He was not tall, but he was trim and broad shouldered, and if you met him on a city street you might conclude that he was a rancher or a miner. If he was wearing his broad-rimmed western hat, wrinkled corduroy jacket, and deputy U.S. Marshal badge, you might think of the old West.

Many years ago an old-time U.S. Fish and Wildlife Service agent gave me his definition of a true outdoorsman. It was simply, "a gentleman in the outdoors." He explained that to him, "gentleman" denoted the kind of person who values the earth's natural areas enough to treat them with the respect and consideration needed to preserve them. Those who have experienced the difficulties, as well as the pleasures, of the way of life in a primitive area may agree that few other environments offer a better opportunity to ascertain the character of a companion. During our fishing trips together, I learned that Max Fleischmann was a skilled angler and naturalist. But during those years, above all else, I realized that he was a "gentleman in the outdoors."

A wish that he will be remembered that way is one of the reasons for the writing of this book.

CHAPTER ONE

Fishing With the Major: The First Year

Maybe almost everyone, before reaching the age of thirty, does something stupid which, in the long run, turns out all right.

The golf course at Glenbrook, Lake Tahoe, was crowded on that July day in 1939; we had waited for almost an hour for our turn to start around the scenic nine holes. Finally the foursome ahead was moving down the fairway, and I stepped up to the driving-line markers.

I was bending down to place my ball when a very large man strode up and nonchalantly pushed a tee into the turf. Adrenaline started flowing, and I was about to say, "Please get your tee out of that grass," when I heard someone call, "One moment." I paused; an elderly man with a tanned, craggy face and wearing a broad-rimmed hat was hurrying toward me. He said, "May I explain something to you?" Extending his hand, he added, "My name is Max Fleischmann."

I had never met Mr. Fleischmann, but like many Nevadans, I felt gratitude for his aid to our university, Boy Scout camp, and other Nevada institutions. His eyes were amused. "I think you were about to take on my playing partner, Max Baer, and I thought I'd better explain that on this nine-hole course, players coming in from their first round have the right-of-way on the tee to complete their eighteen-hole game."

I immediately knew I was wrong, and the adrenal glands returned to normal activity. He introduced me to Baer, and while the big man (who five years before had been

1

heavyweight boxing champion of the world) practiced his golf swing, Major Fleischmann and I talked fishing. I had heard that it was one of his favorite sports, and I saw his interest when I mentioned that I had found a Sierra lake which, with fly equipment, had recently yielded several two- to four-pound Eastern brook trout.

With the foursome ahead out of range, Baer hit a long drive which ended on the edge of the rough. Max Fleischmann followed with a shorter ball which stayed in the middle of the fairway. As he left the tee, he stopped to say, "I'd surely like to fish that lake."

I said, "I'll call you next week."

It was the beginning of many years of fishing together in the western United States, Canada, and Alaska.

And it would not have happened if I had not become angry at Max Baer.

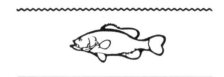

The day that I met Major Fleischmann at Glenbrook and said I would call him about fishing that Sierra lake, I really doubted that the trip would take place. I knew he had fished with many of the great anglers and was known over much of the world for his expeditions and aid to Ducks Unlimited. It seemed absurd that he would go fishing with a schoolteacher who owned a top fly rod only because a sporting goods store had allowed him to pay five or ten dollars a month on it for more than a year.

Major and Mrs. Sarah Fleischmann lived in a large home in the Glenbrook area. I lived near the state line at the south end of the lake in a cabin I had built on a large lot which my great uncle had purchased in the early days when market fishing was legal and land at Tahoe sold for a few hundred dollars an acre. In comparison to the structures they now call cabins in that area, mine should have been called a shack.

In the 1930s there was a small lumber mill off the road to Myers, and I talked the operator into selling me, for ten dollars, enough two-by-four and one-by-twelve boards (very rough-cut and crooked) to build a ten- by fifteen-foot cabin. Tarpaper to cover the roof, screens in place of glass windows, and nails to hold things together brought my total investment to nineteen dollars and seventy-five cents. I had spent my summers before and during college years working for the U.S. Forest Service, and my former district ranger donated a surplus wood-burning cookstove and an ancient iron bed. I built a table, and my needs were satisfied.

About the middle of the week following the golf course encounter, a warm, calm morning indicated good evening insect hatches, and I walked to the nearest pay telephone booth. One of the Fleischmann employees answered, requested my name, and a minute later the Major was on the line. I only had time to say, "I'm going to give the brook trout lake a try this afternoon," when he cut in, "You name the time; I'll be ready."

I drove into the yard about one o'clock; he was waiting on the porch with waders, fly rod, and tackle stacked beside him. Mrs. Fleischmann, apparently in her mid-fifties but still retaining the image of the beauty of her younger years, came out and wished us good fishing. I had a Ford coupe, and with tackle loaded we headed back the way I had come. The "Secret Lake," as Major Fleischmann later named it, was south of the Tahoe basin.

I had forgotten to take along a pair of one-inch-thick by seven-foot-long sticks we would need in crossing an area of bog between solid ground and open water, and I told the Major I would have to stop at my place for a moment. To prepare him for the shock of the cabin's appearance, I mentioned that it was just a shack that I had built for a total cost of nineteen dollars and seventy-five cents. He looked at me to see if I was serious. I doubted that he believed me.

Earlier in the week a neighbor had given me a gallon of old green paint which I had splashed over the rough lumber, and as we drove up to the yard, I thought it looked quite clean and neat. While I was rounding up the sticks, the Major got out of the car and made a circle of the cabin, glancing inside through the open door.

When we started on our way again he was quiet for a few minutes and then said, "That's a compact little cabin. How in the hell did you build it for nineteen dollars?" Well, it took the next twenty miles to explain the transaction because he asked quite a few questions. When I finished I was sure he believed me because he said, "It's a good example of what a guy can do for a little money."

We began to climb the grade out of the basin, the road winding through a forest of beautiful, large ponderosa and Jeffrey pines which the early loggers had left standing. The Major surprised me by saying, "I understand you teach school." I said that I did and that I enjoyed it. He asked, "You also worked for the U.S. Forest Service?" I explained that during college years I had worked as a lookout and fire patrolman and that I still helped on large fires. I did not ask him how he knew about my work, deciding that he had done some background research before going fishing with me.

By three o'clock we crossed the summit of the grade, and the canyon opened into a large meadow surrounding a small lake. It was typical high Sierra country—scattered lodgepole pines, bright green grass, the lake shining in the sunlight, everything looking fresh and clean.

I was paying more attention to the scenery than to the road when a squirrel ran in front of the car. I swerved to miss the little animal, dropped the car's right rear wheel into a rut, and did a short sidewise skid before straightening out. I glanced at the Major; his face was unperturbed; he seemed to be studying the lake and meadow. A few minutes later he said, "I guess you're one of those biology naturalists who don't like to kill animals."

4

I thought for a moment and decided to confess the truth to this famous big-game hunter. "I don't like to kill anything without a reason. I shoot waterfowl and upland game birds which I like to eat. I do enjoy the excitement of the hunt, the beauty of ducks gliding in to decoys. I like shotguns but have no interest in other guns."

The Major then said something which I remember so clearly that I believe I can quote it almost word for word. "On my last trip I shot a water buffalo at fairly close range. They're big animals, and I used a rifle that fires a heavy cartridge. I saw the slug hit him, push him sideways, and it made me wince. That ended my big-game hunting; I put my rifles away. Like you, I still enjoy shotgun shooting."

It was a surprising statement. I was beginning to learn something about Major Fleischmann.

I parked the car out of sight behind some willows and near a small stream which meandered through the meadow down to the lake. We pulled on our waders, put up our fly rods, and I slipped two sandwiches I had made, along with a small canteen of water, into the back pocket of my fishing jacket. The alarm whistling of a mountain quail greeted us as we started following the stream, pausing at a small pool to watch tiny brook trout fingerlings darting across the white sand.

We each carried one of the inch-thick sticks. I had explained that the area we would cross to reach open water was dangerous, apparently consisting of a thick mat of grasses and other plants which was strong enough to hold one's weight but was not solid. I had found several open holes after almost stepping into one of them, and on testing their depth with my eight-foot fly rod, its tip had not reached bottom. The holes did not seem to be more than two to three feet in diameter, and the seven-foot poles carried across the body would prevent submerging beneath the floating mass of plant life.

When we reached the edge of the meadow, the sun was still

above the western mountains, and beyond the marshy area, the surface of the open water appeared undisturbed by feeding fish. I suggested that we wait on solid ground for half an hour and have a sandwich before we started fishing.

He agreed, and we picked a high area along the edge of the trees where we could watch the lake. As we ate we talked fishing—the best flies to use that evening, the larva of the caddis fly (locally called a periwinkle) which I had found to be abundant in the lake, the bright-colored flies like the Parmachene Belle which seemed to be especially attractive to Eastern brook trout. But as the shadows lengthened, we talked less as we watched the beauty which surrounded us. I knew the Major was enjoying these few quiet minutes of relaxation.

He saw the first swirl of a large fish break the surface of the lake, and we quickly got on our way, I leading to avoid the deep holes discovered in previous trips. It was like walking on a thick rubber mat floating on water, and I noticed that the Major was accepting my suggestion to hold the safety stick crosswise to his body.

We were well out on the bog when I saw a car moving along the road just below the summit. Probably the driver was still too far away to see us, and I asked the Major to kneel down behind the tall grass, explaining that, so far, I had found no indication that others knew there were trout in the lake and hoped it would remain that way. When the car had passed by and was out of sight, we continued on to a small bay almost cut off from the main lake by the plant mat.

As we approached the open water, we saw a heavy swirl near an area of large water lily pads. I signaled the Major to try for the fish, and he began false casting his English Hardy rod. His fly settled on the water, and he had started to retrieve when a dorsal fin broke the surface, the Major set the hook, and his reel began spinning.

The fish first headed for open water, but, as I started to feel hopeful, it reversed its run and made for the water lilies. The Major's rod bent almost in a semicircle as he attempted to turn the big trout, but a few seconds later it was over—the fish had tangled the line in thick lily stems and broken the leader. The Major was smiling. I asked him if he wished to move on to the next bay, but he shook his head saying, "I'll let this cool off for a moment and then see if I can lose another one."

I went on about a hundred yards to the next open water, which was deeper. A net was useless because of the danger of standing too close to the edge of the unstable plant mat. To land a fish it had to be tired out and pulled slowly through the grass surrounding the pond.

There were insects above the water, indicating that a hatch was starting, but there were no rising fish, and I guessed they might be feeding on caddis fly larvae as those small creatures struggled towards the surface to complete their life cycle.

I had made a number of casts without a response and was retrieving the line while turning to see if the Major was all right, when something almost took the rod from my hand. A square tail fin lashed out of the water, the broadest I had ever seen in that lake. The loose line raced through my hand, and the reel started clicking. I started to put pressure on the fish as he neared the tall weeds on the opposite side of the pond, and suddenly my fly and leader came shooting back at me. I was wearing the broad, straight-rimmed hat which in those days was part of the uniform of most Forest Service officers, and I took it off and threw it near my feet. The Major never forgot that. Years later when I lost a fish, he would laugh and say, "Why didn't you throw your hat away?"

By the end of the legal fishing day, we both had landed and released several beautiful two- to three-pound trout. The Major had caught and kept the largest, a four-pounder, which would provide a fish dinner. When we drove down the Fleischmann driveway, Mrs. Fleischmann saw the lights of our car and quickly came out to learn what we had caught. She was delighted with the large Eastern brook.

With the Major's gear unloaded, I was about to leave when

he came to my car window and used an adjective which was one of Teddy Roosevelt's favorites. He said, "Mr. Wheeler, it was a bully good trip. Thank you for taking me." I had not yet learned that Major Fleischmann and Roosevelt had been friends.

The beginning of the school year did not allow additional trips that season, but during the winter I received several letters from him. On January 2, 1940, his first letter, written at his newly purchased Hope Plantation near Jacksonboro, South Carolina, began as follows:

My Dear Mr. Wheeler:
I am writing formally, although if I were fishing with you I would not be saying "Mister"—but I'll be darned if I know how to abbreviate Sessions.

The letter ended:
Looking forward to some trips again to our secret place, I remain,

Very Sincerely Yours,
Max C. Fleischmann

In a later answering letter, I made certain that he knew my nickname was "Buck."

CHAPTER TWO

Origins, Business, and the Adventure Years (1877 – 1939)

When we met on the Glenbrook golf course in 1939, Major Fleischmann was sixty-two years old; I was twenty-eight. Although our backgrounds were very different, the outdoors seemed to neutralize any effect that circumstance might have had on our relationship. During the years that we fished together, I felt as much at ease with him as with my lifelong friends.

On our trips we found much to talk about, but unfortunately for this book, he did not discuss his military career, his many expeditions, or the honors he had received. Thinking back, I wonder if he avoided any subject which he feared might make me feel inferior.

I wish that I had questioned him, but I did not, and my knowledge of Max Fleischmann before 1939 had to come from many other sources. Mr. Julius Bergen, the Major's executive secretary for over twenty-five years, contributed the basic information which helped to guide much of the research required to provide an accurate but incomplete story of a man to whom outdoor adventure was a chosen way of life.

Max* Charles Fleischmann was born in Riverside, Ohio, on February 26, 1877, the son of Charles L. Fleischmann and

*His given name was Maximilian, which he shortened to Max.

Henriette (Robertson) Fleischmann. There were three Fleischmann children: Max, his brother Julius, and his sister Bettie (Fleischmann) Holmes.[1]

Max Fleischmann's father, Charles, was born in Jaegersdorf, a suburb of Vienna, Austria, in 1834. As a young man and already an experienced yeast grower, he became superintendent of a large estate in Hungary, where he supervised yeast production.[2]

When he traveled to the United States to attend the wedding of a sister in 1866, Charles noted that there was no commercial yeast production in this country. Most of the bread was baked in the family kitchen with yeast made from potato water, liquid yeast bought by the pint, or with sourdough. It was sourdough that accompanied the emigrants to the goldfields of Idaho, Montana, and Nevada during the mid 1860s. They baked their bread where they camped, and before departing, they often left a lump of sourdough in the crotch of a tree to be certain that the travelers behind them would be able to make bread.[3]

When Charles Fleischmann first tasted American bread, he thought it was inferior to that of his homeland and decided it was due to the yeast. In November of 1866, Fleischmann married Miss Henriette Robertson and returned to Hungary. Two years later, on the advice of his brother-in-law, he again traveled to America accompanied by his brother, Maximilian. As he walked down the gangplank to the land which would be his home for the remainder of his life, he carried in his vest pocket a test tube containing live yeast plants—one-celled living things so tiny they could be seen only with a microscope.

Eventually he took his live yeast to Cincinnati where a prominent distiller, James W. Gaff, became so interested in Fleischmann's idea of manufacturing compressed yeast cakes that he entered into a partnership with the two brothers. With a capital of $40,000, a small factory was built at Riverside, near Cincinnati—the first yeast manufacturing plant in America.[4]

Using a copper vat to hold a malt made from corn, rye, and barley grains and the sugar needed to feed his precious plants, Charles Fleischmann began growing the live yeast he had brought from Hungary. In a relatively short time, the rapidly multiplying organisms had absorbed the extract, and the remaining mixture was then filtered; by a special process, the water was pressed out to leave a smooth paste which was fashioned into cakes.

The production of paper-wrapped cakes of compressed yeast was done by hand, and orders were delivered to customers in baskets. Many American natives were skeptical, but the foreign population, reared on bread made with European yeast, eagerly bought the product. In 1871 the factory building and equipment were destroyed by fire. It was not entirely a disaster—rebuilding brought improved, new equipment which increased output by mechanically cutting the compressed yeast into cakes and wrapping them in tinfoil.

A third Fleischmann brother, Henry, came over from Hungary and on April 26, 1870, established a patent on compressed yeast which he assigned to the inventor, his brother Charles. In 1871 the company constructed another plant in Blissville, Long Island, New York.[5]

In 1876 American inventors, manufacturers, artists, etc. were invited to exhibit their wares at the Centennial World's Fair in Philadelphia. The Fleischmanns and Gaff accepted the invitation, and, in their "Vienna Model Bakery," three million visitors (including grocers and commercial bakers) were allowed to see yeast made, dough rise, and bread baked. Most of the spectators sampled the bread; the exhibition was an outstanding success.

To meet the increased demand for their product, a third plant was constructed at East Millstone, New Jersey, and in later years, the company's largest plant was built at Peekskill, New York.[6]

In 1881 the Fleischmanns bought the Gaff interest in the firm, and on the death of his brother Maximilian, Charles

Fleischmann took over the entire business, operating it under the name of Fleischmann and Company. In 1905 the business was incorporated as The Fleischmann Company.[7]

Charles Fleischmann, a close friend of President McKinley, was elected to the U.S. Senate in 1879. By 1890 Fleischmann had amassed a large fortune. He had an estate in the Catskills, had collected valuable paintings, owned a yacht, and was developing a stable of racehorses which would become the finest in the United States. His success did not change him; he was always simple in style, courteous in manner, and enthusiastic in business. Charles loved music, and after supper at home he would gather his family around the piano, and, while his children sang, he would play (by ear) opera melodies, American songs, and the folk songs of his homeland.

Charles Fleischmann died in 1897 at the age of sixty-three, and only after his death were some details revealed of the things he had done for people. For example, in 1893 he had saved the public of Cincinnati from a loss when the cashier of the Market National Bank absconded with $160,000. Fearing a disastrous run on the bank, Fleischmann took over the loss, accepted a deed to the cashier's home, and after the cashier's death, deeded the house back to the widow.[8]

Max Fleischmann had a fine family background to influence his future life.

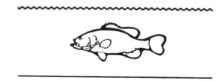

Max received his formal education in the Riverside public schools and at the Ohio Military Institute, where he was an excellent student. He played on Cincinnati's early semiprofessional baseball team and was an amateur boxer. During later life, he was an outstanding polo player and skillful enough at tennis to play with top amateurs. At Lake Tahoe he played with the renowned Helen Wills while she was vacationing there.[9]

I remember the Major telling me of one activity which must have built strong muscles during his teen-age years. We were driving to a Sierra lake on a road which passed by the site of my first job away from home. I pointed out the timbered hillside where, at the age of fifteen, I had dug post holes for a telephone company. He said something about how one of the poles looked crooked and added that he guessed I hadn't been very good at my job. He then said, "When I was about the same age, my father gave me a tour of the yeast factory. When it was completed he asked me what I had found the most interesting. I told him that I enjoyed seeing the big furnaces. For the next year, whenever I wasn't in school, I was put to work shoveling coal into those damn furnaces."

In 1895, at the age of eighteen, Max Fleischmann began working in the manufacturing department of the Fleischmann Company, learning the basics of the family business. Three years later the outbreak of the Spanish American War temporarily interrupted his business career.

On graduating from the Ohio Military Institute in 1896, he had enrolled in the Ohio National Guard, receiving a commission of second lieutenant. When war with Spain was declared in April of 1898, he was commissioned as a second lieutenant in the First Ohio Volunteer Infantry and was soon promoted to first lieutenant in the First Ohio Volunteer Cavalry where he served as acting captain of Company G, First Regiment. Later he was transferred to act as aide-de-camp to Brigadier General Louis H. Carpenter.[10]

Evidence of his ability as an officer during the Spanish American War was found in a recommendation, written in February of 1917, when Fleischmann applied for a commission in the Officers' Reserve Corps. In a letter to the adjutant general in Washington, D.C., Colonel M. W. Day, former commander of the First Ohio Volunteer Cavalry, wrote:

> I have the honor to recommend that Max C. Fleischmann, Cincinnati, Ohio, be given a commission in the Officers' Reserve Corps.
>
> Mr. Fleischmann was a First Lieutenant in my Regiment (1st Ohio Vol. Cav.) and was considered one of the best officers in the Regiment. After being a duty officer he became an aide-de-camp and made an enviable reputation.
>
> I think the Government would be well served by the appointment of Mr. Fleischmann to the position he seeks—especially on account of the reputation he had in the Regiment.
>
> His public reputation shows that he has not gone stale or dead since his discharge from the service and I heartily endorse him for the position.
>
> Very Respectfully
M. W. Day
Col. USA Retired
(Late Comd. Ohio Vol. Cav.)[11]

When the Treaty of Paris ended hostilities in December of 1898, twenty-one-year-old Max returned to his business position, eventually becoming superintendent of the manufacturing department. His intense interest in travel to the primitive regions of the earth resulted in an arrangement where his brother Julius (an astute businessman) became president of the Fleischmann Company, allowing Max, as vice president, more freedom for his expeditions.

On December 20, 1905, Max Fleischmann was married to Sarah Hamilton Sherlock, a beautiful and gracious woman whose enthusiasm for the outdoors matched that of her husband's. Her father, John C. Sherlock, was a retired businessman who had made his home in Cincinnati for many years.[12]

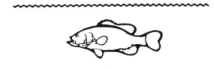

Had he been born earlier in the nineteenth century, Max Fleischmann might well have been one of those who explored the West—one of that kind who had to see beyond the next valley, the next desert, the far mountains.

In the early twentieth century, there still remained regions of the earth which civilized man had not significantly disturbed, and it was those environments which drew the Major across arctic and tropic seas and deep into the back country of most of the world's continents.

Fortunately, his personal diaries of four of his earliest expeditions were preserved when, in 1909, he had them printed in book form.[13] Summarized here, the diaries* are interesting not only for their accounts of adventure but also for the fact that they reveal much about the character of the writer. He titled his first diary "The Cruise Of The *Laura* To The East Greenland Ice-pack."

During the winter of 1905–06, the Major arranged for an expedition to the Arctic which would begin in June of 1906 using a chartered ship, the auxiliary barkentine *Laura*, which was equipped with steam power as well as sails. The first line of his diary characteristically reads, "There was the call of the North behind it all, to begin with."

The objectives of the trip were listed:

1. To approach the Greenland coast near Franz Josef Fjord;
2. If ice conditions permit, to advance north as far as possible toward King William Land;
3. To collect specimens of bird life and study their food and habits;

*The book was not circulated for sale; apparently only enough copies for gifts to friends, relatives, etc., were printed.

4. To attempt to secure live specimens of musk-ox and polar bear;
5. To make short land expeditions.

Although the Fleischmanns had been married only a few months, and though it would be a hard trip, it was decided that Sarah Fleischmann, an experienced sportswoman, would accompany the Major. Also included in the party were Dr. and Mrs. Christian R. Holmes* and son, and Mr. Noel C. Livingstone Learmonth from Blandford, Dorset, England. Later the Major wrote, "The Doctor and I have been criticized for allowing the ladies to accompany us, but neither has since had cause to regret having taken them, they having stood the cruise surprisingly well."

The expedition began at Tromsø, Norway, on June 17, 1906. The diary read:

> Tromsoe Harbor lay bathed in radiance as the *Laura*, flying the New York Yacht Club flag, beat her way out.
> On the dark, rock-bound mountain behind the town ice filled the crevasses. To one side little gabled buildings nestled, as if afraid. A quaint old sailing vessel or two lay in the Bocche; and where the mountains cut off the light, the waters seemed dull and forbidding. Clouds lowered in impressive adieu.

By noon the *Laura* had reached the small island of Skaarø in Fuglø Sound, where, because of a heavy gale at sea, they decided to anchor for two days. The time was not wasted, for the men went fishing for sei—a fish which the Major described as "a gamey fellow, fighting as salmon might, but without breaking water."

The *Laura* set sail on the open sea on June 20. Throughout his diary it is clear that the Major had respect for the captain and crew of the Norwegian ship—with the exception of the chef. Of him he wrote:

*Bettie Fleischmann Holmes, the Major's sister.

Another variant, so early in the cruise, was an intoxicated chef. When, at first, an occasional meal was missed it was not so bad. Things grew worse with toleration, and being no chance to discharge him in favor of some other, the Doctor threatened him with hypodermics so strong as first to make him sick; and then, should he drink again, to kill him. The threat worked remarkably well.

On June 21 the ship reached Bear Island and the first large masses of floe ice. Here the Major began collecting specimens and observing the habits of bird life—a scientific study he continued throughout the journey.

Two in the morning of June 22nd, when finally we sailed from Bear Island, the midnight sun—a ball of fire just over the skyline, all its radial lines cut by the fog—created a scene which baffled the pen for its beauty. Distant icebergs near the sky line glinted and glimmered, while the drift ice, on which two seals appeared, was heavier than is usually found here.

Progress was slow, necessarily; the sea grew heavier, and sharp snow flurries accentuated a thermometer at 33 degrees [Fahrenheit].

That day and the next the waters lashed wild. Half past five in the morning our rudder unshipped. Although we secured it, there was no anchorage nearer than Spitzbergen for repairs, so that we were forced to employ a makeshift and continue, with the rudder astern, at the rate of one to three knots an hour. Welcome, indeed, was Spitzbergen when sighted [in the distance] at half past seven.

Our rudder incident was not yet closed. The day following the accident, the tow ropes became entangled in the propeller, and we had to lay to several hours to free it.

On June 24 the ship reached a sheltered bay east of Spitzbergen's southernmost cape, and here the rudder was repaired.

Spitzbergen (Svalbard) is a group of islands in the Arctic Ocean belonging to Norway. The largest of the islands, West Spitzbergen, is approximately 15,000 square miles in size; the total land area of the entire group is 24,293 square miles.

For the remainder of the month of June, the *Laura* traveled along the coast of West Spitzbergen and among many of the islands, anchoring in some of the bays to collect birds and other animals. Time was also spent preparing the collected specimens which eventually would go to Berlin for tanning and then to the United States for mounting.

The Fourth of July was spent at the point of Danes Island in Virgo Bay, where the Wellman expedition (sponsored by the *Chicago Record-Herald*) had established its station.[14] It had also been the departure site of the ill-fated Andrée expedition.[15]

> On Independence Day, sure enough, we lifted our hats to Old Glory. . . .
>
> Mr. Wellman not being present (though being expected in a very few days) and neither firecrackers nor fireworks being at hand, U.S. Army Major Hersey, second-in-command of the polar expedition, ordered a salute by a squad armed with pistols, guns, and the like; which we returned in kind.

On July 7 the *Laura* continued on. "Early morning brought us within six hundred miles of the Pole. . . . It was evident that, thanks to the solid ice remaining till late, we could get no further north." The next day the "real seal region was reached; cries of 'Kobbe! Kobbe!' (seal!) sounded again and again from the crew."

The following days were spent collecting various species of seal and arctic birds. What the Major called a "rather exciting experience" occurred when one of the small boats carrying the Major's party of seal hunters became lost in a heavy fog among thick ice floes which threatened to separate them permanently from the ship. For a while, even the sound of the *Laura*'s fog horn was blotted out, but when they were again within its sound, they were able to reach the ship.

On July 18, the diary read:

> Heavy fog, rigging ice-covered, mercury at zero, formed the setting to our ship, forced to buck savagely now in trying to win a passage on, to fairly open water beyond.
>
> Ever and always, also, we must guard against being hemmed in. In the course of this butting the ice plates were wrenched from their bolts and partly separated from the wood on the port bow.
>
> The *Laura* beginning to take water at the rate of a foot an hour now, double forces were necessary at the pumps, while we lightened the ship foward, so as to raise her sufficiently to permit the carpenters to stop the leak.

On July 19 a polar bear was shot, their first specimen of that large northern carnivore. They continued on, attempting to find passages through the ice, and on July 26 the air cleared enough for them to see from the crow's nest the coast of Greenland, seventy-five miles distant. Solid ice barred the ship from the coast, and attempts to bore the pack were unsuccessful. From July 27 "until the 20th of August, the *Laura* was enveloped in fog, or else beset—front, rear, and sides—by ice floes."

During this period a polar bear cub was captured by pursuing it in one of the small boats. The cub showed remarkable strength. After a noose had been slipped over its head, it towed the boat while growling fiercely, striking at the gunwale, and sinking its teeth into the steering pole. However, after being placed in a cage on the ship, it ate a meal of seal blubber and showed a liking for sugar. Later, "Tommy," as he was named, "resigned to his fate, and munching at sugar or swilling a thick dried-pea soup, with manifest content, made an interesting playmate."*

*Tommy went to the Cincinnati Zoological Gardens where he grew to become a splendid specimen of *Ursus polaris*.

"Finally the truth would not be downed—we would probably not get to Greenland." During one memorable hour, the ship had reached a point within twenty-odd miles of the coast before the ice pack again blocked the way. On August 20, with coal running low and "realizing the inevitable, we set sail for Jan Mayen, after having cruised up and down the relentless pack, between Latitudes 73 degrees and 78 degrees, for six weeks or so."

By the evening of August 21, the ship was clear of the heavy ice, and during the next two days the *Laura* proceeded full sail on her way to Jan Mayen,

> a queer spoon-shaped island, thirty miles long by twenty-three at its broadest. . . . On the island, a house which was built for an Austrian meteorological expedition in 1882 still stands.
>
> Before leaving Jan Mayen we landed our Bos'n and two men, together with a large quantity of provisions. The three were to spend the winter trapping, as well as taking meteorological observations in the interest of the Norwegian government.

The men were to be recovered the next year, but later Major Fleischmann learned that when, in 1907, the *Laura* became icebound in the Greenland pack, another ship was sent for the men. "After picking them up she was beset by ice and storm and sank with all but one of her seventeen hands. By queer play of fate, moreover, the *Laura* escaped the ice and called at Jan Mayen not forty-eight hours after the relief ship's departure."

On August 28 the coast of Norway was sighted. "It seemed odd, indeed, to see houses, trees, meadows and cattle, when, at seven that morning, we cast anchor at Tromsø."

Later, in his introduction to his diary, Major Fleischmann wrote, "As to time hanging heavily on our hands, in regard to which we are often asked, and as how we managed to amuse ourselves, . . . so far as the writer is concerned, there was not one dull moment during the trip."

Within two months of his return from the Arctic, Max Fleischmann was arranging another expedition, the diary of which was titled "On Safari Through British East Africa."

In addition to the diary written during the African trip, the Major later wrote an article for the September 1907 issue of *Cosmopolitan Magazine* titled "An Up-to-Date African Hunt." It was preceded by the following editor's note:

> This article is a personal narrative of a remarkable hunting trip made by a venturesome young American whose love of sport and practical ingenuity in seeking it will appeal to every reader of the *Cosmopolitan.* In the summer of 1906, Mr. Fleischmann, with his bride, made a honeymoon trip to the polar regions, which was immediately followed by the journey to the interior of Africa described in the following pages. The ease and rapidity with which this was performed is a startling reminder of the progress of development in the Dark Continent. As we go to press there comes a report that Mr. Fleischmann is presently to undertake a long journey by balloon.

The following summary of the expedition is largely based on Major Fleischmann's diary, but includes several more explicit accounts from the *Cosmopolitan* article.

The party included Major and Mrs. Fleischmann, Archibald Kennedy (a Fleischmann employee), and the Englishman, Noel C. Livingstone Learmonth, who had been on the Arctic trip. Leaving London by train on February 15, 1907, they arrived at Marseilles the next morning in time to board the steamer, *The Admiral,* which carried them in nineteen days through the Suez Canal, Red Sea, Gulf of Aden, and Indian Ocean to Mombasa on the east coast of Africa. During a stop at the town of Aden, two Somali shikaris (first gunbearers) had come aboard, their employment having been previously arranged because of their dependability and a reputation of not knowing "the meaning of the word fear."

The expedition was to be confined to British East Africa, with most of the big-game hunting done in the region of the Thika and Tana rivers, the Embo country, and around the foothills of Mount Kenia (Kenya).

On March 7 the party left Mombasa for Nairobi on the Uganda Railroad train, an overnight trip in cars equipped with leather benches on which passengers could sleep if they provided their own bedding.

In Nairobi, the group "put up at the Norfolk Hotel, a hostelry known to sportsmen all over the world and very excellently conducted."*

The Fleischmann safari, which had been previously arranged, consisted of sixty-five natives, including a headman, four gun-bearers, a cook, four askaris (native soldiers), six horse-and-donkey boys, three servants, and forty-six porters. Wages ranged from eighty-five rupees (one rupee equaling about thirty-two cents) per month for the headman to ten rupees for a porter.

On March 9 the safari got underway, reaching the Thika River the next day. With the two sportsmen hunting ahead, the caravan moved downstream, reaching the junction of the Thika and Tana rivers on the eighteenth. During the march a wounded wart hog charged the Major, who killed it at a distance of less than ten yards. Four days later, while he was attempting to photograph a rhinoceros with a calf, the mother charged him, and he was forced to drop the large animal with a hurried shot at about fifteen yards.

In the *Cosmopolitan* article, the Major stated his general opinion that, with the exception of the rhinoceros, African animals did not charge a man unless wounded or cornered.

---

*Sportsmans Safaris, Inc. of Reno, which arranges trips to Africa, states that the Norfolk Hotel is still operating and enjoying the same reputation Major Fleischmann described in 1907.

He said there were records of a rhino charging safaris, "and in one instance a rhinoceros charged and hit a train on the Uganda Railroad."

It was on March 18 that the Fleischmann safari experienced an event which received the attention of some of the world's major newspapers. The London *Times*, in a two-column story, credited Max and Sarah Fleischmann with having "witnessed a spectacle in the wilds of Africa which no other human being has ever beheld, and at the same time having photographed the previously unheard-of contest between a rhinoceros and a crocodile."[16]

Major Fleischmann's account in the *Cosmopolitan* magazine follows.

> It was at the junction of the Thika and Tana rivers that we witnessed a fight between a rhinoceros and a crocodile. The rhinoceros had come down to the river to drink, and, while it was standing about knee deep in the water, a crocodile grabbed the big animal by the left hind foot. Then ensued a tug of war. The saurian backed toward deeper water, and the monstrous rhinoceros was exerting all its strength to get back to shore. It was powerless to use its horns, its only weapons of defense, and you can imagine the size of that crocodile when I say that it pulled the rhinoceros out into deeper water and down-stream for a distance of over one hundred and fifty feet.
>
> Our party was on the bank watching the fight with feverish interest and sympathizing with the rhinoceros, but the rhinoceros did not win out—the battle was unequal. The water soon became discolored with blood, which showed that other crocodiles had been attracted to the spot and were beginning to make a meal off the rhinoceros. But the end of the rhinoceros had not been far off when reinforcements for the crocodile began to arrive, and very soon the huge carcass disappeared beneath the water. It was one of the most remarkable sights I have ever beheld.

The safari reached Fort Hall on March 22 where they camped for the night on Government Square and dined with a Mr. Lane, Sub-Commissioner of the Kenya district. Mr. Lane estimated "the total white population of British East Africa to be only one thousand souls."

On March 24, after sending a consignment of trophy skins back to Nairobi, the safari headed for the Embo country—arriving at Fort Embo on the twenty-sixth and continuing down the Rupengazi River to make camp in beautiful, open country. While the Major was out hunting, "a rhino approached within one hundred yards of the camp, on a run, but was frightened off by Kennedy, the askaris, and porters; Mrs. Fleischmann taking to the 'tall timbers'—in other words, making a brave attempt to climb a thorn tree."

March 30 turned out to be a good day for Major Fleischmann. Hunting Cape buffalo in a heavy thorn thicket, he came upon a herd just as it broke across a small clearing.

Managed to get a fine head—fifty and one-half inches spread on the curve. It was really a remarkable stroke of luck, as the specimen secured turned out to be the record head of British East Africa, although, when I pulled the trigger, I had absolutely no idea that I was shooting at the best animal within range.

On April 5, the safari returned to Fort Embo. Shortly after arrival there,

a chief came in with a bodyguard of four hundred Kikkuyu warriors, and it was one of the most imposing sights I have ever witnessed. Each wore a headdress of aigret or ostrich feathers, while over the shoulder was thrown a leopard's skin or the skin of some other animal. Each wore a breech-cloth and had a steel band around his ankle. The men were well drilled. At a signal from the chief they would step in unison, and the steel bands would jingle musically. At the same time they would shift their spears, and the sun's rays would glance from them, making a very pretty spectacle.

The next day the safari started for Fort Hall, making camp about halfway.

> The cook being short of meat, we went out for guinea fowl, which had been seen near camp. Greatly to the amusement of the beaters, I fell into a muddy river and returned very shortly; but between us we managed to get enough birds to last as food until we reach the game country again.
>
> Learmonth, ailing for some time, the result of over-taxing himself in the Embo country, became quite ill with dysentery on our arrival in camp, and took to bed. . . . Ali, the headman, and the cook visited his tent, praying and making mystic signs over his cot to remove evil spirits.

On April 8, the safari left Fort Hall for lion country in the vicinity of Punda Milia. While hunting ourebi, a species of antelope, the Major came upon a newly born one, "about three hours old, and it came all the way home with us. We made a feeding apparatus for the little animal out of pipe stems, and then sent a runner fifty miles to get a nursing bottle." Within a week, "M'Toto, our baby antelope, was eating grass and taking milk from a saucer."

While hunting lions,

> our sport was devoid of any great danger. . . . In one instance we were, perhaps, particularly fortunate in that we found a lioness with a cub in high grass. Instead of attacking us, under these circumstances, as it was generally supposed she would do, the lioness started to run away, leaving her five months old cub to be captured alive by our little party. . . . the shikarees, following the cub through the waving grass, soon captured the little fellow. [The only casualty during the capture was] Hirsi, the shikari, [who] received several ugly scratches in making a football tackle on the beast. He was ren-

dered helpless when I threw a coat over his head, and will join the animal colony at the Cincinnati Zoo.

On April 21, on returning to camp, the Major found runners with a letter stating that the steamboat agent had made a mistake and had no accommodations on the ship the party was supposed to take on May 10. Deciding they might do better by immediately getting to Nairobi and then Mombasa, the camp was broken at daybreak.

In one and a half days, the safari marched forty-eight miles to Nairobi, where the work of disbanding the safari, sorting and packing the trophies, settling financial affairs, and making a cage for the lion cub was rushed through in two days.*

Reaching Mombasa on April 27, they sailed at midnight aboard the German East African boat *Kanzlar*, a dilapidated tub to be retired from passenger trade on arrival in Hamburg at the end of that voyage. "A cargo of copra and green hides wafted 'perfume' our way, but success during the two-months shooting and our luck in not being held up, a month or so, awaiting a steamer, prevented this dampening our spirits in the slightest."

Arriving in Genoa two days ahead of time, the Major ended his diary with, "Our luck, evidently, was still holding good—concluding for us a most enjoyable, as well as most successful, African hunt!"

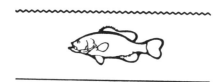

By springtime of the next year, "The Call of the North" was tempting Fleischmann again. His diary of this expedition was titled "By Pack Train Through The Cassiar."

---

*The Cincinnati zoo received three live animals from the Fleischmann expedition—the lion cub, the baby antelope, and a kangaroo cat of the lemur family.

On August 12, 1908, the Major left New York bound for Victoria, B.C., on the first step of a rugged journey. The stated purpose of the trip was to obtain a specimen of *Ovis stonei*, the stone sheep.

At the Empress Hotel in Victoria, the Major was met by Mr. Clifford Little, who was to accompany him as companion and guide. Their acquaintance had been only through correspondence,

> hence it was not without some trepidation that I met the gentleman who was to share with me the pleasures and hardships of the lone Northern country for many ensuing weeks. The best, or the worst, side of a man's character is almost sure to come out when "hoofing" it along the trail—sometimes wet, sometimes hungry, sometimes disappointed; so that taking a trip of this kind with practically a stranger is a great deal of a gamble. However, after a half hour's chat with Little, I felt my choice to have been a wise one, and I am happy to say that subsequent acquaintance more than proved my estimate true.

On August 19, the Major and Little were on the veranda of the Empress Hotel awaiting the arrival of the ship, the *Princess Victoria*, which would carry them to Vancouver. There they would transfer to the ship, *Beatrice*, for the trip to Wrangell, Alaska, and the Stikine River. The *Victoria* was scheduled to remain in port one-half hour and give a five-minute whistle before leaving.

The two men watched the ship dock and saw Fleischmann's employee, Archibald Kennedy, already aboard with the Major's luggage. Believing they had ample time, Fleischmann and Little delayed walking to the ship until they heard the sound of the whistle. When they reached the dock, the *Victoria* was in midstream—it had not whistled until the lines had been cast off.

> Our feelings are hard to describe; personally, thirty cents would have been a high value to place on my own

inward observations. There was Kennedy on board—with all my baggage, letters of credit, and, in fact, everything I had brought from home with me. It was absolutely a catastrophe, since missing this boat meant we could not make connections with the boat up the Stikine River—our destination. What was more, the [Stikine] vessel makes only two trips a year.

Hurrying back to the hotel, they received the full cooperation of the manager, whose efforts resulted in their traveling by motor car, train, and chartered ship, as well as telephonic communication with Kennedy. At two o'clock the next morning, they caught the *Beatrice* at Vancouver, Kennedy having transferred the baggage to that ship. Major Fleischmann wrote, "It is said that 'all's well that ends well,' but if Little or myself dies before the age of three-score and ten, I believe one reason for it can be put down to a certain few hours passed this day."

The *Beatrice* arrived at Wrangell on August 24, and on the twenty-sixth Fleischmann and Little boarded the Hudson's Bay Company steamer *Hazelton* for the 150-mile trip up the Stikine River.

Four days later, after getting stuck on sand bars and stopping to chop wood for fuel—work in which the passengers as well as the crew participated—the ship reached Telegraph Creek, a Hudson's Bay Company post with a store, commissioner's office, saloon, several warehouses, and a population of twenty whites and about one hundred Tholtan Indians.

Here the trek would begin, and the next several days were spent in completing their outfit, which included provisions, five pack horses, and two Tholtan Indian guides, Bob Reed and John Colbert.

The Major was favorably impressed with the two Indians.

These two fellows take great pride in their strength and endurance. We heard from absolutely reliable witnesses that in a weight lifting contest, Colbert had lifted eight hundred pounds on and off the scales, and that he carried ten sacks of flour, weighing fifty pounds each, up a very steep hill.

They have a very keen sense of humor, also.

Again, no work is too hard for them so long as it be concerned directly with getting game.

On August 30 the pack trip began, following the old Ashcroft Trail to Buckley Lake, a distance of thirty-two miles. On September 1,

after conference with the Indians, we decided to leave the Ashcroft Trail and head southeast, endeavoring to cross the range [Cassiar] a little north of the headwaters of the Iskoot; thus traversing a section of country where, if we are fortunate in striking good weather, we shall have a fine chance of securing bear. While this route will be a great deal rougher, and entails crossing three complete mountain ranges, we shall reach our objective—the Kappan River—about the same time as if following the Ashcroft Trail, and it will not be such monotonous traveling.

During the next two days, "Progress was slow, we passing over extremely rough country, and this amid a constant downpour of rain." Their camp on September 3 was a wet one. But they had killed a porcupine along the way and enjoyed it as a stew for supper. Throughout the trip, the game animals and other species obtained along the trail provided an important part of their food supply.

The next morning started with a

terrific hailstorm, followed by intermittent snow flurries and showers. Our horses' backs were too wet to permit packing, so we decided to await more settled weather for crossing the next mountain range. Instead of lying around camp, however, resolved to try the peaks behind us for sheep. After what was to me a rather heartbreaking climb, in a blinding snowstorm, we reached the summit, and for an hour were forced to shelter behind a rock. Here we ate our pilot-biscuit and cheese, hoping, the while, that the weather would clear, in order that we might use our binoculars in searching the hills.

Finally this happened, and very soon we sighted two goats [Rocky Mountain goats], some distance below us. Stalked to get within shooting range. I shot, hitting one hard back of the shoulder. . . . Made a rather bad shot on the other, hitting too far back.*

The first goat, showing more signs of life than I liked, I then ran in pursuit of it, asking Little to finish off the second, which he did, knocking it over in one shot.

Both goats were big fellows, their horns measuring ten-and-a-quarter and ten-and-seven-eighths inches in length and six-and-one-half and seven inches at base, respectively.

During that night their tent collapsed from four inches of snow on the canvas, and the storm continued during the day. The Indians managed to shoot a fat ground hog for supper, which was roasted on a spit before an open campfire.

On September 7, under cloudy skies, the party was packed and underway early in the morning, hoping to cross Fog Mountain and the headwaters of the Iskoot River.

On reaching a high altitude . . . the sun would be shining one moment; a miniature blizzard would envelop us the next. It was very cold on the mountain tops, and we packed over mile upon mile of perpetual snow, which held up under our weight though making rather hard traveling for the horses. When, from time to time, the sun did appear, the panorama which unfolded was magnificient beyond what a hunter's pen should attempt to describe.

---

*Many hunters might hesitate to admit a poor shot, let alone record it for posterity. Throughout the Major's diaries he includes his embarrassing moments, showing his lack of self-importance and self-deception.

Later in the day they saw five black wolves, and the Indian, Colbert, called to them.

In fact quite a "howling fest" occurred between the Indian and one wolf, who appeared to be the spokesman of the party. A deep corrie separating us, both parties appeared to invite the other to come across and visit. Neither accepted the invitation, and after perhaps ten minutes of singing, the other Indian, Little, and I burst out laughing so heartily that the entire party broke up.

The stone sheep range, where they would hunt that game animal, was still far away when, the next morning, they came to a lake which blocked their route. After making camp, they cut twenty-four-foot logs which were tied together to form a raft capable of transporting their packs. The Major and Colbert poled the raft several miles to a point where they met Reed and Little with the horses, which had swum across the lake.

Packed and proceeded through the broken timber slowly, crossing a morass where four of the five horses were bogged, one or more times apiece, and where to make crossing at all possible, it finally became necessary to remove their packs and carry [the packs] across on our backs; we leading the horses over later on. The language of the Indians—and possibly of the rest of us, at times, was hardly the fit sort to print.

Wet blankets and a pouring rain which "drenched us to the skin" resulted in an uncomfortable camp that night. "We are nearing the sheep grounds, however—a very consoling fact, and one buoying up our dampened spirits." A day of marching under a steady drizzle of rain finally brought the party to the foot of the mountain where sheep could be found. Here they made camp to await clearing weather, the mountains being covered with clouds and mist.

It was windy but fairly clear the next morning (September 11), and the Major, Little, and Colbert headed up the mountain.

After a terrific climb, came across fresh tracks of a band of rams which we proceeded to follow till unfavorable wind compelled us to change our direction.

Left the tracks and went over the top of the peak, approaching the sheep from the other side. Later saw them feeding down toward timber-line. The position was unfavorable for a stalk, but we determined to do the best we could. Taking advantage of any shelter in our path, and crawling in the open spaces, we managed to get within fair shooting distance of them. The wind, which was very puffy, must have swerved, or else we had been seen while stalking; for the rams were already moving off when Colbert poked his head over the ridge, and by the time I came up, he was unable to shoot to advantage. I too leveled my gun several times—but was so fagged by the stiff climbing and the running, that a film gathered before my eyes, the muzzle wavered, and I could not draw a bead.

I decided not to shoot at all. . . . I have always hesitated at shooting unless reasonably sure of some result.

After a short rest we decided to climb, up over the snow line, and attempt again crossing the tracks of the band.

The Indian dropping suddenly while on this climb, we followed his example, when with our glasses we again discovered the sheep about one thousand feet below us at the foot of the precipice, and at the side of the opposite mountain. Evidently they had not been very much frightened—having caught glimpses of us only when we stalked down mountain toward them; and so, failing to catch our wind, they had merely grown restless.

Their new position was a most favorable one, and after a very easy descent, I managed to bag three—the limit of my license—before the herd made off.

One of these proved a most excellent specimen, forty-four inches full on the curve; twenty-five-and-a-half inches spread; and fourteen inches in circumference at the base of the horns.

The wind was extremely raw and it was very cold on

the mountain top, so we wasted no more time than necessary.

Returning to camp, we must have come within fifty yards of a grizzly, for we heard him crashing through the bushes; but the wind being unfavorable, he scented us, while the thick brush prevented our getting sight of him.

We dined sumptuously this evening on a whole side of a sheep, roasted before the fire. The meat was excellent.

They decided to spend the next day in camp resting and preparing the heads and skins. Rain and fog settled in early and kept up most of the day. "However, no one has minded the weather; all are jubilant at our having obtained the large sheep-head, which we have measured accurately and find to be the record *Ovis stonei* killed in the Cassiar to date."

They broke camp the next morning to pack toward the Ashcroft Trail, heading for the caribou country beyond the Kappan River. After traveling about eight miles, they set up camp again to give Little an opportunity to get his sheep.

On September 14 they awakened to a light, frozen fog. Little and Colbert went up the mountain, while the Major,

having secured my limit of sheep and feeling very well satisfied, I crawled under the blankets again. About eight o'clock we heard four shots, so I sent Bob up the mountain to help bring in any meat which might have been taken, while I remained behind, washing dishes, cutting firewood, and (it having cleared in the meantime) laying out the skins, as well as performing all other chores necessary to camp.

Our hunters returned late in the afternoon with two sheep, both very good heads—thirty-four and thirty-six inches, respectively.

The next morning dawned foggy but the sun forced its way through the clouds, and the party continued on towards the

Ashcroft Trail. Progress was slow, with considerable trail cutting. "Incidently, the nature poet who writes of the 'aroma of the woods' at early morn ought to mush behind five pack horses, eating bunch grass, and he would change the tenor of his ditty!" Along the way they saw a band of twelve rams. Little could have taken one more on his license, but felt he had enough and so did not disturb the sheep. Much trail cutting was again required the next day, and when they made camp all were so tired that "Little and I shall not trouble to blow up our air mattresses, being quite sure of resting on the bare ground."

The party reached the Ashcroft Trail on September 17.

> This trail was the scene of innumerable tragedies during the Klondike rush of '98, and even today discarded camp-outfits, pack-saddles, skeletons of horses, etc., may be seen—mute witnesses . . . to the privations and hardships endured by thousands of tenderfeet . . . who ventured into the wilderness at that time without faintest knowledge of what was necessary in camp outfit and the like.

Further along the trail they made a cache of their trophies by stripping a tree of its bark (to make it difficult for animals to raid the bundle) and building a platform among its branches. The cache would be recovered on the homeward trip. The next day, when they reached the Kappan River, they were one hundred miles in a direct line from Telegraph Creek. During the march they shot three ducks and two porcupines, which they cooked into a stew that evening.

On September 21, they awakened to find several inches of snow on the tent. Breaking camp, they had a stiff climb crossing a mountain range. "The view from the mountain top—the white peaks stretching off, apparently interminable—was wonderfully beautiful, particularly since atmospheric conditions were just right for seeing a great distance. We were able to recognize one peak off, at least seventy-five miles, toward the Stikine."

They reached the caribou country the next day and made "the snuggest camp we have made to date—warm and cozy, with the Indians singing the 'Caribou Song' of the Tholtan tribe." En route to the campsite, they had seen a large herd of caribou, on which they made a stalk, "crawling over the snow a long time flat on our stomachs. It was a pretty sight, this, and we lay watching the herd until we were numb with cold, when we made a move which set them off, at their awkward, shambling gait—a pace which does not appear [to be] very fast but which chews up distance, nevertheless."

On September 24 they were to have a long, hard hunt over mountains and heavy snow.

> We had risen early—stiff and sore in every joint. Received little sympathy from the Indians, who thought our discomfiture a huge joke.
>
> About five miles from camp we saw a herd of caribou, and this we proceeded to stalk. Went up a corrie, burning grass ahead of us, in order to do away with the taint in the wind. I am told by the Indians that caribou and mountain sheep are the only animals who do not fear the odor of smoke, and who, therefore, can be approached—down wind, by grass being burned ahead of the stalkers.

There were no good heads among those bulls, but later they sighted another herd, with trophy-antlered bulls, disappearing over the crest of the mountain. After several hours of hard climbing, they were able to approach the caribou to within shooting distance and obtained good heads. Later the Indians took the horses and brought in the meat.

The next day was spent skinning and cleaning the head skins and resting. Late that afternoon, snow began falling, continuing through the night. With a heavy wind, the storm kept them "snowbound" in camp for two days. On September 28 Little secured "a magnificent caribou, one of the finest ever brought out of the Cassiar." It was now time to start the return trip to Telegraph Creek.

As the homeward bound "trek" begins tomorrow [September 30], we remained in camp today to fix up scalps secured, shoe the horses, go over our pack-saddles, and attend the other details relative to an early start.

As we are about ten days' march from Telegraph Creek and expect to spend two or three days looking for moose enroute, we anticipate arriving there between the 12th and 14th; i.e., the time originally set.

A light shower bade us God-speed about nine this morning, and by four-thirty we had completed a most satisfactory day's march, making a distance which required two days to cover on the trip "in."

The next day's journey was considerably different. After wallowing through a cedar swamp and thick willow brush, the Major wrote, "To go into particulars of this day's travel would force one to language he should much prefer to omit. I might add, though, in justification of the above, that during the day's march our pack-horses were bogged and mired not less than nine times."

On October 5, they reached the site of their cache and added its contents to their packs. Five days later, they were within twenty-five miles of Telegraph Creek.

Rose before daybreak, breakfasted, and started packing by moonlight. The men having about finished with this, Little and I started ahead at dawn to pick up grouse and duck on the sloughs some distance ahead 'longside the trail.

It was a glorious morning, and as the sun burst forth and began to pour its rays on the snow-capped mountains stretching off toward the Stikine, and upon the pine forests round Buckley Lake, nearer by, a panorama was presented which, once seen, is never to be forgotten! On such a day as this, all the discomfiture of rain and fog and snow is forgiven, if not forgotten!

Camped some twelve or fifteen miles from Telegraph Creek. Little knocking down five grouse and two mallards, we had a "big feed" tonight.

On October 11, being in a hurry to reach town, Fleischmann and Little used what they called "the one-man pony-express" method. Little left camp on their one saddle horse, riding as fast as possible. After covering about one mile, he dismounted, tied the horse, and proceeded on foot at a jog or fast walk. On reaching the horse, the Major mounted and galloped a mile past Little where he dismounted, tied the horse, and continued down the trail on foot. "This procedure was followed until the landing across the river from Telegraph Creek was reached. By means of it two men can make very good time with but a single horse."

When the Indians and pack horses arrived at Telegraph Creek, Little's caribou head and the Major's largest stone sheep received much admiration. After being measured by the government commissioner, the sheep was entered as the record head for the Cassiar.

The following four days were spent in Telegraph Creek awaiting a war canoe (built by the Haida Indians) which would carry the two men down-river to Wrangell. It was an enjoyable four days for the Major—talking to the prospectors who were on their way out of the wilderness to work during the winter and earn a grubstake for the next year's prospecting. He also went to the Indian village to watch a native gambling game where a participant guesses in which hand his opponent is holding a stick.

On the night before leaving for Wrangell, the town gave Fleischmann and Little a farewell dance at Hyland's warehouse. The Major wrote, "The ball last night was a great success, everybody dancing in moccasins. It would really be a splendid plan to follow this custom at more civilized functions, since with it a poor dancer can step with impunity on his partner's feet, and no injury result from such awkwardness."

They started down-river at seven-thirty the next morning with a crew of four Stikine Indians (a Tlingit people), including a Carlisle graduate and ex-halfback, George Snake, as captain. The Major was impressed with the skill of the Indians. "The manner in which the Indians handled the canoe, in certain strips of water, was marvelous. When making time, or when striving to gain some eddy where power is required, they employ a very trying stroke, rising from their seats with each such pull, so as to bring the full force of their weight on the same." The trip required the better part of three days, with two overnight stops. Snow, rain, and hail fell during most of the second day. On October 18, they landed at Wrangell—eight days short of two months since they had boarded the steamer *Hazelton* there for the trip up the Stikine.

Max Fleischmann arrived in Victoria on October 25, where he ended his account of the hardships and adventures of the rugged trip with the same thought he had written in his African diary: "The end of a most enjoyable and successful trip."

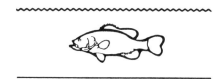

Although the Cassiar had provided more than the main motive for the expedition—a record stone sheep—Max Fleischmann had hoped to also obtain an Alaskan brown bear. So, it was not surprising that during the winter of 1908, with the aid of Clifford Little, he entered into correspondence with the proprietor of a general store in Wrangell to arrange the chartering of a motor launch with which he could reach the neighboring islands in search of this animal—the largest carnivore on earth. He titled his diary, "After Alaskan Bear."

On April 30, 1909, approximately six months after returning from the Cassiar, the Major and his party—consisting of
Mrs. Fleischmann, Little, and an employee, Jules Vincent—
sailed from Seattle aboard the steamer *Cottage City*, arriving
at Wrangell, Alaska, on May 3.

The forty-five-foot motor launch, *Taku*, with a Captain
Lancaster, an engineer, and an Indian named Barney who
knew the islands, arrived from Ketchikan on May 6. The
Fleischmann party boarded the *Taku* the next morning and,
after an overnight stop at Peterburg, arrived the next day at
Eliza Harbor, Admiralty Island. Barney went ashore to visit
an Indian encampment. There he was told that six bears had
been seen at Chopin Bay the previous day—about a thirty-
minute sail away.

The Major wrote in his diary:

> When, about the beginning of May, bear come out of
> their holes after hibernating all winter, the question of
> something to eat is naturally the all-important one with
> them. Nature has so provided that the only foods avail-
> able at this time are skunk cabbage and grass. These
> seem not only to satisfy the pangs of hunger succeeding
> the long winter's fast, but also to act as a purgative, and
> to put Bruin in fine fettle for beginning his salmon joys.
>
> By the end of June or early July, this search for food
> becomes a simpler matter, since all the streams teem
> with salmon. The island bear being a fish eater to the
> exclusion of almost everything else, morning and eve-
> ning brings him to the riffles and shallows over which
> the fish are running, and there, with little effort, he
> catches and eats his fill.

Unable to locate bear at Chopin Bay, they returned to Eliza
Harbor where they spent several days of industrious but
unsuccessful hunting. Moving on to Pybus Bay, they sighted
a big female bear and a cub on a snowfield high up on a
mountain. Apparently the bears had just come out of their
den and were attempting to cross the mountain crest. "After

climbing and wallowing in the deep snow, sometimes lying down to rest before trying still once again, they finally gave up and returned to the haunt where first we had seen them."

On May 16 they sailed to Baranof Island and into several of its bays and then returned to Eliza Harbor where Barney guided them on a long inland trip. Their only luck that day occurred when "Mrs. Fleischmann caught a fine mess of crabs near the boat; most delightful eating, these." Returning to Pybus Bay, their fortunes finally changed for the better.

> Had no luck on the morning hunt; but this afternoon we came upon a three-year-old male, feeding on a grassy swale. Being in a most disadvantageous position for stalking, we removed coats, hats, and boots, and crawled through the bushes to get within range—i.e., one hundred and forty to one hundred and fifty yards.
>
> I shot, and the bear dropped like a log, the shot being aimed back of the elbow. As the animal did not stir, we, of course, supposed him dead. Sent Barney for our boots, while we kept the prey covered—the rest of us not going out at once to him, since the grassy spot, dotted with sharp rocks, where he lay, was separated from us by a mountain stream, making boots almost a necessity.
>
> The bear being dead, it would be foolish to rush at him in any discomfort. Barney returning and the bear still showing no signs of life, we proceeded to don the boots. While in the very midst of these doings, the "dead" bear suddenly came to life, and, starting off through the water and into the thick woods on the jump, his back alone showed for a target.
>
> A couple of our shots hitting him, we followed the trail up the hill. The bear could not travel rapidly, so we caught up to him and finished our work, less than a quarter of a mile from where he first had been sighted.

On May 21, Fleischmann, Little, and Barney started at 3:30 A.M. on a full day hunt, with the launch to meet them at the end of the day in a cove further up the Pybus. "Hunted all morning, rowing some eight miles up-stream and making a noon hour stop on a small island. Having taken only a light lunch along, a mess of clams, which Little and I dug out with sticks and then steamed over some sea weed, formed a welcome addition." Late in the afternoon the hunters started for the cove settled on as rendezvous. Not seeing the launch, they decided that the engine must have suffered a breakdown.

However, Mrs. Fleischmann and the others had arrived at the cove somewhat earlier, and finding no sign of the hunters, feared they might have mistaken the meeting place. They decided to search in nearby coves, and in one of the small bays they spotted a large brown bear. Taking the one and only gun aboard the *Taku*, and with Captain Lancaster rowing the launch's small boat, Mrs. Fleischmann stalked the bear and, at a distance of 175 yards, brought it down with one shot. "Though much elated, now that they had killed their game, our friends did not know what to do with their quarry, and so commenced their search for us, returning to the original cove at last. Here they picked us up; all returning then to skin the carcass."

Content with their specimens of the Alaskan brown bear, they proceeded to Kupreanof Island, which Barney recommended as a good black bear hunting area. On May 31 and June 1, they collected two of these smaller bears, and, "satisfied now at the result of our hunt, we desiring not the accumulation of a big bag, but a few specimens of black and Alaska brown bear alone, we were ready to turn ship homeward now." The party left Wrangell by steamer on June 4. In Seattle, two days were spent viewing the Alaska-Yukon-Pacific Exposition, which "served as a pleasant finale to this 'cruise after bear in a motor launch.' "

Unpublished diaries of many of Major Fleischmann's journeys, known to have existed, have not been found; it is believed that after Mrs. Fleischmann's death they may have been discarded. Records do show that in 1910, Fleischmann again went to Africa and was in the vicinity of Mount Marsabit and the border of Abyssinia (Ethiopia). Two years later he was in Asia's Altai Mountains and Outer Mongolia. In 1914 he made an expedition to northeastern Rhodesia.

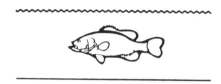

In between expeditions Max Fleischmann evidently was a conscientious and capable businessman. In his 1912 book, *Cincinnati, The Queen City,* Charles F. Goss stated that Fleischmann understood his company's business and, in addition, was a director of the Market National Bank, and vice president of the Illinois Vinegar Company, the Fleischmann Malting Company, and the American Diamalt Company.

Goss wrote that Fleischmann took a great interest in the Masonic Order and had the thirty-second degree; he was a member of the Blue Lodge and chapter commandery and was also a Shriner. Socially, he was quite active as a member of the Queen City Club of Cincinnati and was a life member of the Benevolent and Protective Order of the Elks. "He is fond of outdoor diversions . . . and has many warm, personal friends in the organizations with which he is connected. In business he has been remarkably successful for one of his age and ranks among the most energetic and progressive men of Cincinnati."[17]

In addition to outdoor interests, Max was one of the country's early aircraft enthusiasts. In 1909, under the auspices of the Aero Club of America, he won the Lahm Cup with the free balloon *New York* on a flight with Holland Forbes from St. Louis to the Atlantic. He held Hydroaeroplane Certificate No. 46, dated April 12, 1916, and Spherical Balloon Pilot Certificate No. 67, dated July 11, 1917.[18]

Apparently Fleischmann anticipated the United States entering the war with Germany, and on March 28, 1917, he applied for a commission as captain in the Signal Officers' Reserve Corps, Balloon Division. An April 3, 1917, letter from the chief balloon instructor of the United States Army Balloon School to the chief signal officer of the army, read:

> 1. It is learned that Mr. Max C. Fleischmann has applied for commission as Captain in the Balloon Branch of the Aviation Section, Signal Officers' Reserve Corps. His appointment in the Reserve Corps is most heartily endorsed.
> 2. Mr. Fleischmann has made a number of free balloon flights with me and is fully qualified as a spherical balloon pilot. In addition to his ballooning experience it is understood that he is also a qualified aviator and has considerable military experience.[19]

On May 15, 1917, Max Fleischmann's application, which had been approved by the examination board of the Signal Officers' Reserve Corps, was approved by W. T. Johnston, Adjutant General of the Army.

Undated orders from the National Archives indicate that Max Fleischmann was promoted to major and was stationed at Vadenay (Marne) and Cuperly (Marne), France. In addition to becoming commandant of the Army Aeronautical School at Vadenay, Fleischmann was assigned other responsibilities. For instance, one order dated February 18, 1918, read, "Major Max C. Fleischmann, A.S., S.O.R.C., will proceed to the Headquarters of the 2nd and 6th French Armies, and such other places as may be necessary, for the purpose of observing the operation of captive balloons. Upon completion of this duty, Major Fleischmann will report to the Chief of Air Services."[20] Later, Major Fleischmann was put out of action by an enemy gas attack, and when he was sufficiently recovered from the effects of the poison gas, he was transferred to the United States to become commandant of the U.S. Army Balloon School at Arcadia, California.*

During their marriage, in addition to the Cincinnati residence, Max and Sarah Fleischmann had homes for short periods of time in Greenwich, Connecticut; Sands Point, Long Island, New York; and an apartment at the Park Lane in New York City. While stationed at Arcadia, they drove to Santa Barbara where they were so impressed with the beauty of the area that, in 1921, they bought property near the city, built a home, and began developing an avocado and lemon farm which they named Edgewood Ranch. In Santa Barbara they soon became responsible and respected residents.

In 1925, when the Major was on an expedition in the White Nile region of Africa, Julius Fleischmann died of a heart attack while playing polo in Florida. On March 11, 1925, the *New York Times* reported:

> Major Max C. Fleischmann, brother of the late Julius Fleischmann, who received news of his brother's death by runners in Africa, arrived here yesterday.... He went from the ship to the Fleischmann Company offices ... where at a special meeting of the Board of Directors he was elected Chairman.
>
> Major Fleischmann, who has hunted big game in every part of the world, was on a hunt in equatorial Africa when his brother died in Miami on Feb. 5. The cable was sent to the French Government with the request that Major Fleischmann be sought at once. The whereabouts of the party was not exactly known, so the French officials dispatched several boats and more than a score of runners with copies of the cable. Major Fleischmann was found five days later just as he was starting for a day's shoot, and he turned back for the coast, whence he took a boat for London and arrived here a month after receiving the message.

*A fire at the National Personnel Records Center at St. Louis in 1973 destroyed the remainder of Major Fleischmann's military record.

Because the Major preferred to live in Santa Barbara, the Fleischmann Company requested Julius Bergen, who had been secretary to Julius Fleischmann, to move to Santa Barbara to become executive secretary to the new chairman.

In 1929 The Fleischmann Company merged with other companies under the new corporate name of Standard Brands, Inc. The Major retired from active service as board chairman, although remaining a director until 1942 and retaining an advisory position as chairman of the Finance Committee of Standard Brands until his death. He was the largest individual stockholder of the company, and he kept in touch with developments, which required periodic trips to New York. (In 1981 Standard Brands combined with Nabisco, Inc. to form the current company, Nabisco Brands, Inc.) From 1926 to 1934, in order to carry out business responsibilities, the Major owned a private railroad car in which to make the necessary trips to New York offices, and in 1935 he purchased a two-engine Lockheed airplane, which greatly reduced his travel time. Although the Fleischmanns traveled extensively, Santa Barbara was their home from 1921 to 1934.

In 1951, a Santa Barbara newspaper editorial titled "Major Fleischmann Invested In Community's Future" summarized his fourteen years in that city. Parts of the editorial follow:

> To some men who inherit or acquire great wealth is given the added boon of a deep sense of responsibility and the imagination to invest in things of enduring value. . . .
>
> Many of the things, both tangible and intangible, which make Santa Barbara a place of beauty and congeniality, with educational, cultural and recreational opportunities for all people, are due in whole or part to the generosity of Major Fleischmann. But his generosity was not of the casual kind.
>
> The gift without the giver is bare—and The Major lived by that truth. He did not customarily "give," he

invested. He invested in the future development and enrichment of this community, of which for many years he was a member, though he traveled extensively and lived elsewhere. He invested not only in such tangible things as the Breakwater and Yacht Harbor, the Polo Field, the Museum of Natural History, Cottage Hospital, the Valley Club and St. Vincent's School.

He invested in the spirit of adventure and search for scientific truth and enlightenment exemplified by the expeditions and progressive program of the Museum of Natural History. He invested in the love of music and the joy of participation, in the development of talent and character of youth, by his continuing benefactions through the Santa Barbara Foundation.* He invested in the vigorous life of competition and fair play on the gridiron, on the polo field, and in other realms of sport. He was virtually godfather to the Dons of Santa Barbara High School, giving a helping hand in many quiet, little ways that were never made public.

In all these varied investments, the money he gave was only part of the whole; he gave of his wisdom and experience in planning, in following through with administrative problems and details; his specialized knowledge in many fields and his ability to see with a broad vision and work with practical efficiency oftentimes was even more valuable than the actual money. His sponsorship gave assurance to other public spirited citizens that the projects or programs he was associated with were soundly based and would be productive of lasting benefit.[21]

Probably the Santa Barbara Museum of Natural History occupied more of the Major's time than any one of his many

---

*In 1928 Major Fleischmann invited twenty-five civic-minded men to meet and draw up articles of incorporation for a Santa Barbara Foundation, a community institution. Fleischmann gave 3,500 shares of capital stock of Standard Brands Corporation, and later additional gifts, to the Foundation.

other projects. He became interested in the museum around 1925, and in 1927 he was elected a member of its board of trustees. In 1929 he was chosen to be vice-president, and in 1934 he accepted election as president.[22]

During the years he served in the various offices, the museum almost tripled in size. The Major's first gift was the Mammal Hall, along with an endowment to support the Department of Mammology. In 1929 the Fleischmann Trophy Hall was built and used as the museum library; it eventually would contain his private library on natural history and his collection of game animal specimens obtained from many parts of the world. In 1934 the Major and Mrs. Fleischmann helped to plan for and financed construction of the museum's most well known section, the Sarah Hamilton Fleischmann Bird Hall, and adjoining laboratories. The hall contained one of the best displays of its kind in the country, and the exhibit's beauty and scientific value made it a favorite of visitors. The large Fleischmann auditorium was completed in 1938 to provide a hall for lectures and exhibits and a meeting place for interested groups. Large as it was, the lecture courses sponsored by the Museum Association taxed its capacity. Much of the Indian material which decorated the auditorium's walls was collected by the Fleischmanns during their many cruises to Alaska.

Major Fleischmann was genuinely interested in the activities of the museum staff. Attending their weekly meetings when he was available, he enjoyed sitting at the big table in the library where tea was served during lively discussions of experiences of the staff members.

Believing that he should not continue as president of the museum beyond his seventieth year, the Major retired in 1947. At the urging of the board, he agreed to take over as executive vice-president and remain on the board of trustees. In 1950 he resigned from the board to devote more time to his interests in Nevada. The trustees prevailed upon him to accept election as honorary president for life.[23]

Major Fleischmann loved the sea, and during his lifetime built twenty-two yachts.[24] The first may have been the auxiliary yacht *Haida* in which he made a cruise in 1903. He named his ships for the Haida Indians of the Queen Charlotte Islands—a tribe known for their seafaring ability. In their great dugout canoes, ranging up to seventy feet in length and decorated with brightly colored paintings and carved animals, the Haidas sailed among the islands off the British Columbia coast to attack enemies and visit with friends. Undoubtedly, the Major admired these skilled early American seamen.

Berthed in San Pedro harbor, the Fleischmann yacht was readily available for his many trips to Alaskan and southern waters. The Major received much enjoyment from fishing, and as a naturalist, he was interested in studying and classifying the various species caught during his cruises. Especially on his trips to Mexican waters, "often accompanied by better-than-amateur ichthyologists," he had found a great diversity of opinion about the classification of certain species and, although using the best reference books, was unable to identify many of them.

On meeting Dr. Lionel A. Walford, a marine biologist associated with various government agencies—including the U.S. Fish and Wildlife Service—the Major planned a cruise in the 127-foot current *Haida* for the purpose of developing a book which would make a contribution to scientific knowledge of marine game fishes of the Pacific coast. In March and April of 1935, Fleischmann led the expedition of three scientists and five anglers to Mexican Pacific waters. The *Haida* was equipped with a laboratory, aquarium, photography equipment (including a darkroom), fishing tackle, and small boats. The anglers were able to keep the scientists busy studying, photographing, and painting the fish which, when possible, were brought to the *Haida* alive. During the two months, five new species were discovered and described for the first time.

The expedition provided much of the material in Dr. Walford's large and excellently illustrated book, *Marine Game Fishes of the Pacific Coast From Alaska to the Equator,* a contribution from the Santa Barbara Museum of Natural History. It was published in 1937 by the University of California Press (Berkeley) and Cambridge University, London.

CHAPTER THREE

The Nevada Years (1935 – 1950)

In the early 1930s, changes in the California tax laws prompted a number of Major Fleischmann's California friends to establish residence in Nevada. In 1934 the Major concluded that they had made a wise decision, and he began the process of acquiring property at Glenbrook, Lake Tahoe, and building a residence. He retained his Edgewood ranch near Santa Barbara, usually spending several months there each fall and spring. This arrangement, and additional trips for board meetings, allowed him to continue as president of the Santa Barbara Museum of Natural History.

Moving to his new home in 1935, he soon found that Nevada offered the type of life he enjoyed, and eventually he acquired three additional holdings: the 200,000-acre Morgan Ranch in Mason Valley, the 30,000-acre Jacks Valley Ranch, and the Ladino Dairy Farm south of Reno.

It was not long before he had become a helpful citizen in civic, community, and statewide activities. The Boy Scouts of northwestern Nevada benefited greatly when he participated financially in building a summer camp which they named Camp Fleischmann. His ranching interests brought him in touch with the agricultural services at the University of Nevada, and after becoming familiar with the needs of the university, he provided substantial endowments for scholarships and gave his previously acquired Ladino property to the institution as a complete, operating experimental dairy farm. Other organizations received financial aid as well as his help in other ways. In business matters, he was one of the organizers who established the Security Bank of Nevada. He liked Nevadans, and they liked him.

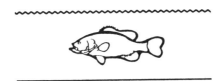

Over the years, the Major had contributed specimens to the American Museum of Natural History in New York City, and in 1936 he and Dr. James L. Clark led the museum's scientific collecting expedition to Indochina. Articles in the museum's magazine, *Natural History,* and the *New York Times* provide a brief sketch of the journey.

On February 14, 1936, the *New York Times* reported:

> Because many forms of wildlife in the interior of Indo-China may become extinct, the American Museum of Natural History is sponsoring an expedition to gather as many specimens of jungle life as possible. Dr. James L. Clark, director of the museum's department of arts, preparation, and installation, will leave today for San Francisco where he will meet Major Max C. Fleischmann . . . who will head the expedition. . . .
>
> The party . . . will spend about two months in the jungle and steaming swamps of Indo-China. A special effort will be made to capture specimens of the tiger and wild buffalo.

According to the museum's *Natural History* magazine, headquarters were established at Saigon in March, and automobiles transported the party and local guides three hundred miles into the jungle to a small community called Dong-Me. Here a camp and field laboratory were set up, and during the next two weeks, an excellent collection of local birds, snakes, bats, and lizards was obtained. From Dong-Me, excursions on foot (often twelve to fifteen miles under hot temperatures) resulted in the collection of several specimens of the banting, a wild ox resembling a domestic cow. Specimens of wild pig were also obtained.

Moving southward to the Lagna River and the broad, grassy plains of that great wildlife region, bullock carts replaced automobiles to carry supplies over rough trails into the jungle. A base camp was established on the banks of the Lagna River among large trees and elephant grass. Here, specimens of wild water buffalo, seladang (a massive wild ox), hog deer, mouse deer, and numerous reptiles and fishes were collected. Although the spoor of tigers indicated those animals were plentiful, the hunters were unable to obtain a specimen before the torrential monsoon rains arrived, requiring the expedition to start homeward in order to save the valuable collection from deterioration. In Saigon, the specimens were packed for shipment to the museum.[1] Reporting the return of the expedition, the *New York Times* wrote, "Sizes of specimens, Dr. Clark said, varied from the giant water buffalo weighing 3,000 pounds to the mouse deer which weighed only four pounds."[2]

In 1938 Major Fleischmann, accompanied by his wife, Sarah, returned to Indochina to collect specimens, primarily tiger, for the American Museum of Natural History. Hunting in Cambodia, they were successful, and Mrs. Fleischmann obtained her own fine tiger. It was the Major's last big-game hunt.

Major Fleischmann's expeditions were acknowledged both nationally and internationally. He was elected a Fellow of the Royal Geographic Society of London and was a life member of the Explorers Club in New York. He was a member of the Arctic Club and was one of the few fifty-year members of the New York Yacht Club. He also served as president of the Western Museum Conference. Because of his active interest in conservation, Fleischmann was elected a director of Ducks Unlimited in Canada and a trustee of the Save-the-Redwoods League. His expeditions were in some way related to providing additional knowledge of the living things of the parts of the world he visited, and his trophies and collections either went directly or eventually to museums or other scientific institutions.[3]

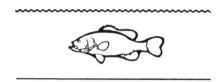

Undoubtedly, museums were one of Max Fleischmann's special interests, and the story of the Major's participation in the development of the Nevada State Museum in Carson City is an example of the time and energy—in addition to financial support—he was willing to devote to a project he had decided to aid.

Construction of Carson City's United States Mint began in September 1866; it began functioning on January 6, 1870, and terminated its minting operation in 1893. The building, constructed of local sandstone, was used for assaying until 1933, when it was completely abandoned. In the summer of 1938, Judge Clark J. Guild, a grand old Nevadan, was walking past the deserted structure when he noticed a sign on the building which read, "For Sale, Procurement Department, United States Treasury."[4]

Judge Guild stopped to gaze at the familiar old landmark, and as he stood there the thought came that the building could be made into a museum—the first Nevada State Museum. Continuing on his way home, the Judge met a close friend, George Sanford, and he paused to mention his idea. Sanford, an attorney, was immediately interested and suggested that they determine the selling price by sending a telegram to U.S. Senator Pat McCarran of Nevada. An answer arrived the next day stating that the appraised value was six thousand dollars. Encouraged by the reasonable amount, the two men again wired McCarran, requesting that he attempt to put a bill through Congress enabling the state of Nevada to purchase the building at the appraised value for a state museum. The senator cooperated, and in record time an enabling act was passed by Congress.

The Judge went to work contacting in person or by letter most of the service clubs in the state, and Nevadans quickly rallied to his appeal for support. A bill was drafted for the upcoming biennial session of the state legislature, and on March 25, 1939, an act incorporating the Nevada State Museum and appropriating funds to purchase the mint building was passed. Governor Carville appointed William Donovan, Miles Pike, and Judge Guild to the museum's board of trustees.

The new board faced a formidable task, but the Judge was up to the challenge. The building's roof, in a deplorable condition, was leaking, so he contacted the Kennecott Copper Company at McGill, the Consolidated Copper Company at Kimberly, and the Mountain City Copper Company. The three firms cooperated to put an excellent copper roof on the new museum. Funds for renovation were needed, and Judge Guild, through personal solicitation, raised approximately three thousand dollars in gifts from George Wingfield, Hal Lennon, and several of the clubs and hotels in Reno.

In 1939 the federal Works Progress Administration was instituting public work projects to relieve national unemployment, and the Judge contacted the director for Nevada. After considerable negotiation, a project was established to help renovate the building, with the museum furnishing the material and the WPA providing the labor.

For many years Judge Guild had been a friend of Lester D. Summerfield, Major Fleischmann's Nevada attorney. One day Lester called to say, "Judge, you have a wonderful idea. Why don't you get in touch with Major Fleischmann? That's his hobby, and he did wonders for the museum in Santa Barbara." The Judge wrote Fleischmann and two days later received an answer. The Major would have nothing to do with it.

The Judge's son, well-known Reno attorney Clark J. Guild,

Jr., remembers that in the fall of 1939, while he was recovering from an automobile accident and confined to a bed in his father's den, Major Fleischmann came to the house unannounced. Through the open den door Clark could see the Judge usher the Major into the living room where, after tossing his broad-rimmed hat on a chair, he turned to the Judge and said, "I've been down looking at that monstrosity that you acquired. You don't know anything about a museum or how to operate it, but I admire your courage in going after it." Before leaving, the Major unexpectedly made an appointment to see the interior of the building.

The following Sunday the Judge guided the Major through the old mint's various rooms, explaining how WPA workers were removing office partitions and installing wallboard to cover the whitewashed stone walls. When the tour was completed, the Major turned to the Judge and asked, "What do you know about a museum?"

The Judge answered, "I don't know anything, but, by gum, I've been around; I've been to large cities; I've been to many museums. This may be a dream of mine, but I hope to see it consummated if everything I can do will help do it."

The Major was silent for a moment and then said, "Judge, I like your guts, and I'm going to give you five thousand dollars to get started. I told Governor Carville, when the bill was before the legislature, that they couldn't do anything with this building as a museum, and if the state would appropriate $150,000 I'd match it. But let's see what you can do. I want you to be my guests, you and Mr. Donovan, down to Santa Barbara for two or three days and see what makes a museum tick."

Several weeks after the trip to Santa Barbara, the Major, on his way to Lake Tahoe, stopped at the museum and walked through the rooms where work was in progress. He did not stay long, and when he reached his Glenbrook home he telephoned Judge Guild and said, "Judge, I want you to bring Governor Carville and the museum board up here tonight. I want to talk to you." The Judge was worried by the Major's request, feeling that something was wrong, but with the governor and the other members of the board cooperating, the group arrived at the Fleischmann residence that evening.

It did not take long for the Major to get down to business. "I was in the museum this afternoon on my way to the lake. I stopped to see what you were doing. I was just completely disgusted. There was one man standing there rolling a cigarette. There was another man sitting in a chair watching a man drill holes in the wall. If you can't do better than that, forget it."

The Judge said, "Well, Major, that's all we can do with the money we have."

The Major said, "It's not all you can do—fire them."

The Judge asked, "And then what do we do?"

The Major was ready with an answer. "I'll put my contractor up there and finish the job."

With the enthusiastic approval of the board and the governor, Major Fleischmann completed the renovation. It cost him about nineteen thousand dollars. The museum was dedicated on State Admission Day, October 31, 1941.

But the Judge's dream had not yet been entirely fulfilled. The basement of the building, where during the mint's operation bullion and coins had been stored, was ideal in several ways for the building of a life-size display which would be a prototype of a Nevada gold and silver mine. Judge Guild broached the idea to Bill Donovan, who had been a mining man throughout his adult life, and he then contacted Jay Carpenter and Vincent Gianella of the University of Nevada Mackay School of Mines, John C. Kinnear of the Kennecott Copper Company, and Nevada mining men Louis Gordon and Roy Hardy. All were unanimous in the belief that the exhibit would be unique and a tribute to the mining industry of the state.

The Major had been persuaded to accept an honorary directorship of the museum, and, during the months he lived in Nevada, he never missed a meeting of the board. The mine idea immediately caught his interest, and he arrived at one of the meetings with three cigar boxes fastened together and filled with plaster of Paris through which he had drilled holes. Presenting his creation, he asked, "Judge, is this what you are trying to do in the basement?"

The Judge smiled. "Major, were you ever in a mine?"

"I never was in a mine in my life."

The Judge said, "Well, you're going in one very soon. The meeting is recessed—Donovan, take him up to the Silver Hill and New York Mines and show him what a mine is."

About a week later, Judge Guild's courtroom phone rang. The court clerk answered it and handed the Judge a note which read, "Major Fleischmann wants to talk to you. He's at the museum." The Judge excused himself to the attorneys and went to the phone. The Major said, "Judge, I want you to come down to the museum right away. I've got Walter Dorwin Teague, the great designer from New York. I want you to talk to him."

The Judge explained, "Major, I'm holding court."

The Major said, "The hell with that court. This is more important."

So the Judge recessed the court until one-thirty instead of the usual one o'clock and went to the museum. There, after introductions, the Major said, "Judge, I want you to get a driver and a car, and I want Mr. Teague taken all around the state of Nevada to show him what mines are. We're going to have him build a model here of what we want."

The Judge called Bob Allen, the state highway engineer, and Allen willingly provided a car and a driver. The next day Teague was on his way to Ely, Tonopah, Goldfield, Pioche, Gerlach, The Getchell Mine in Humboldt County, and Virginia City. He arrived back at the museum in about a week with many photographs and told the Judge and the Major that he could build a model for them in about four months.

The Major asked, "How much is it going to cost?"

"Between ten and twelve thousand dollars."

"Well," the Major said, "get busy right away."

The Judge was stunned. During the past few years, from clubs and hotels around the state, he had raised about twelve thousand dollars and he thought, "Here goes my money."

The model was completed on time and taken to the Utah State Fair and then to the museum. Major Fleischmann paid the cost of the model, and when Teague arrived with it the Major asked, "Can you duplicate this model down here in the basement, and how much will it cost?"

"Oh," Teague said, "take a year or two and probably cost a hundred and fifty thousand dollars."

The Major said, "Well, we'll think it over."

The Judge discussed the cost with the mining men he had previously contacted about the display. They said, "Judge, that's ridiculous. We'll give you all of the ore out of all of the mines that you want—cinnabar, gold, silver, copper, lead, zinc—but you'll have to put it in place. We'll bring it right to the museum yard. We'll give you all the timbers, all the rails, everything you want, but you'll have to put it together." Louis Gordon and Roy Hardy both said they thought the mine could be built for less than fifty thousand dollars.

When the Judge's report was made at the next meeting of the museum board, the Major listened carefully and then said, "If you think you can do it, go ahead. Here's thirty-five thousand dollars to get you started."

At the beginning of the large and difficult project, Jim Calhoun, a practical miner with considerable experience, was hired as museum director, and the Major obtained the services of the Santa Barbara Museum of Natural History's chief technician, Phil Orr. Many Nevadans backed the project; the cooperation was excellent. Ore was brought in to the museum yard from many of the state's mines, and some operators provided ore cars, rails, and machinery. The I. H. Kent Company of Fallon and the Oliver Lumber Company of Carson City each furnished a carload of lumber; old timbers were gathered from the mines in Virginia City; Attorney Jack Ross (later a U.S. Judge) donated a hoist, and other individuals helped in various ways.

Without ever interfering, the Major spent much time at the museum, helping wherever he could. The mine project became his main interest, and he followed every step of the work. Putting the ore back in place so that it was similar to the way it had been in the mines was a technical, tedious, and difficult process. It took two years to accomplish the Judge's dream, which the Major shared, but the mine was opened and dedicated on October 31, 1950.

Judge Guild wrote, "And on that day, it would have done your heart good to see Major Fleischmann directing the tour of the people—and there were thousands of them going through the mine. He enjoyed that mine more than anyone else, I think, other than perhaps Donovan and I. It was part of him. He gloried in it. And what a tribute to a wonderful philanthropist, a wonderful man."

With the mine completed, the Judge was interested in starting a collection of birds, mammals, fish, and the other living things of Nevada. A fine naturalist, Mrs. G. C. Mills of Fallon, had a collection of birds, and the Judge invited the Major to drive with him to Fallon to see it. The Major was skeptical, saying that the birds probably had been shot by an amateur and damaged, but he agreed to the trip just for the pleasure of riding with the Judge.

Mrs. Mills had a fairly large room almost covered with the mounted birds, and the Major was surprised by the professional quality of the taxidermy. After carefully examining them he said, "Mrs. Mills, why don't you put these where people can see and enjoy them? . . . If you'll give them to the museum, I'll have my carpenter build cases for them." Mrs. Mills presented the birds to the museum, and she was voted Honorary Curator of Ornithology. From that beginning, the museum built its bird collection.

According to an article written by David W. Toll in the *Nevada Highways and Parks* magazine (Fall 1968), Major Fleischmann provided the museum a total of eighty-six thousand dollars in cash and two hundred thousand dollars in stock during his lifetime. Undoubtedly these totals do not include the salaries he paid his carpenter and the technicians he brought from Santa Barbara.

The museum's files contain a letter from the Major, a part of which tells something about his character, in addition to his dry sense of humor. Addressed to a secretary, Ms. Dayton, he wrote:

> I note your last letter was written on a new letterhead on which my name appears as Honorable Max C. Fleischmann, Honorary Director. I feel very much flattered by that, now being Director General of the Nevada State Museum and Honorary Director, but I'll be damned if I am an Honorable Max C. Fleischmann.
>
> I might be a Major, and I might be every other thing, but I never was called Honorable in my life. So blue pencil that. . . .

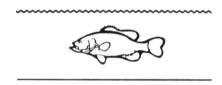

During the fall and winter months of the years Major Fleischmann and I fished together, we corresponded periodically—writing about our current bird hunting, discussing the Ducks Unlimited organization in which we were both interested, and sometimes making plans for the following summer's fishing trips. In rummaging through my old files, I have found some, but far from all, of his letters. In some instances they have helped to relate our fishing experiences to the years in which they occurred.

On March 11, 1940, he wrote in part,

> I am sending you a few flies that I want you to try next year with the idea that I found them very successful, and I think they should be good on Char. Lately I have been using the Hay fly quite a lot and never before had

them in small sizes. When I fished up in Quebec, where there was nothing but Char and Eastern Brook trout, we used a cast of Parmacheene Belle, Scarlet Ibis and Montreal, and it just occurred to me that I am going to have a few of those flies for us to try.

I never went back to the lake again except for the trip we had together as I did not want to take a chance with too many people going up there giving the place away. . . . But I look forward to us having a few good days up there, and it ought to be pretty good sometime in June.

On June 24, I had a card from Mrs. Fleischmann. "Dear Mr. Wheeler—The Major returned today. Had a successful trip. He hopes to see you soon and is looking forward to an outing with you." On July 8, Mr. Julius Bergen, the Major's executive secretary wrote,

Before taking off for Denver this morning, Major Fleischmann asked me to advise you that the little collapsible boat had arrived. He expects to return here probably on Wednesday and hopes you and he will be able to go out on Thursday or Friday.

I wish you would let me know your proper initials for my record. Also have you a telephone number at which you could be reached? You might let me have this by return mail.

It was during our first trip together the previous summer and through correspondence that winter that we had decided to try the main lake connected to our "secret place." Most sensible anglers would be more than satisfied with the two- to four-pound Eastern brook trout we had caught the year before, but when I mentioned my unscientific hypothesis that "the larger the water, the larger the fish" the Major could not resist the possibility of record fish inhabiting the lake. My cabin did not have anything as luxurious as a telephone, but somehow, toward the end of the week, we were headed down the road with a large unopened carton labeled "Collapsible Boat" protruding from the trunk of my Ford coupe.

It was about an hour before sundown when we unloaded the carton and carried it down to the edge of the water. Opening one end, we pulled out a roll of waterproofed canvas along with a hinged, wooden contraption. There was a set of directions which the Major read aloud as, step by step, we assembled the parts. Strangely enough, they quickly formed a boat about eight feet long with two seats and a pair of jointed oars. I looked at it and wished that I had brought along the two life preservers which hung on the wall of the cabin. The Major asked, "Do you think the damn thing will carry two people?"

I shrugged, "Apparently there's only one way to find out, but let's do it in shallow water."

We assembled our rods, decided not to use waders in case we had to swim, and launched the "Queen Mary." I held the gunwales as the Major climbed in, and he steadied the craft with the oars while I crawled cautiously over the side. Surprisingly, it floated with about four inches of freeboard.

The Major rowed slowly out on the lake; I looked over the side expecting to see bottom—there was only dark, deep water below us. Fortunately, the surface of the lake was like glass, but both of us knew that a sudden wind would swamp us. We started paralleling the shore, hoping that we were within swimming distance of it.

The Major began casting, dropping his small fly lightly on the water while the line was still in the air. It was about the same time of evening that fish had begun surface feeding at our secret place, but watching the surface of the lake in the distance and in all directions, I could see no disturbance of its smoothness. We tried a Parmachene Belle, a Montreal, a Scarlet Ibis, and even an imitation periwinkle fished below the surface. We tried the shallower water and the deep. We might as well have cast a bare line.

As daylight faded, an evening breeze began rippling the surface, the tiny waves wetting the canvas closer to the gunwales. We headed for the landing area. With the boat repacked in its carton, we started for home—I, feeling sorry that the Major had wasted money on the small craft. But as we dropped down into the Tahoe Basin, he said, "Buck, our experiment didn't work out, but I enjoyed every minute of it. We had all of the anticipation of catching a big fish, and that is half the fun. And I'm glad we tried it, or we would have always wondered if we had passed up something. How about hitting our secret place next week?" I agreed.

As before, Mrs. Fleischmann met us when we drove into the yard. Our story brought a knowing smile.

I'm sure there is a moral to this story—something about being satisfied with a good thing. But as far as fishing is concerned, I do not believe in it.

We made several trips to our original ponds, always catching nice fish; and in August I received word from my long-time fishing companions, Harold Curran, Clayton Phillips, and Ralph Rhodes, that Red Lake, on the Carson Pass highway, was starting to produce.

The Major and I again shoved the collapsible boat into the trunk of my Ford and headed for Rhodes's camp. Ralph (we called him the mayor of Red Lake) lived in Gardnerville most of the year, but when Eastern brook trout started feeding on Red Lake in late summer, he moved there with tent, stove, bed, and a metal boat. Ralph had been an officer in World War I, and it was not long before he and the Major were conversing on friendly terms while I assembled the "Queen Mary."

Harold and his wife, Virginia (my sister), and Clayton and his wife (another Virginia) arrived. Harold and Clayton were to use Ralph's boat. Their wives planned to visit with Ralph and take a walk along the shore.

As the sun began to slip behind the peaks guarding the pass named for John C. Frémont's famed guide, Kit Carson, dimples began appearing on the lake's surface as the evening hatch of insects started fluttering over the water. Trout began rising, and in seconds the Major's fly rod was bending with the pull of a fifteen-inch Eastern brook. The frantic feeding did not continue long, perhaps twenty to thirty minutes, but it was great while it lasted. We kept a few of the larger trout, releasing the others. It was getting dark as we landed our tiny craft on the shore in front of Ralph's camp.

Clayton and Harold came on shore as we dismantled the boat, and we all agreed that it had been a good evening. Ralph suggested that we return soon and use his metal boat. We set a date—but if we had been able to look into the future, I'm not certain we would have accepted his invitation.

It was about the middle of the next week that we pushed Ralph's boat off the shore and began rowing to the far end of the lake where the western mountains were beginning to shadow the water. Considering the high elevation, it was an exceptionally warm and humid afternoon with puffy cumulus clouds beginning to tower above the peaks. There was no wind, and as we reached the shadowed area, we saw trout rising. The fishing was excellent—often we both had a fish on at the same time. But as the clouds, with their dark, flat bases, moved over us, I felt concern. I could see the Major also watching them, and I said, "It looks like a thunderstorm; maybe we had better start back." He nodded, and I took the oars and headed the boat for Ralph's camp.

We had reached the middle of the lake when the first heavy gust of an east wind, being sucked toward the rising air of the storm, hit us. In seconds the quiet surface was whipped into whitecaps, and rain, lightning, and thunder began. A jagged streak of lightning attached itself to the top of a dead tree on shore, and the instantaneous clap of thunder sounded like a giant cannon. A metal boat wasn't the safest place in a lightning storm.

The wind had reached such a velocity that we were making little or no progress, and the crests of breaking waves were throwing spray over the gunwales. The Major called, "Let me take one of the oars." Because of his age, I believed I could make better progress alone, but he was climbing back to sit beside me.

During the following years, I never again worried about him being too old. It took every muscle in my back, arms, and legs to stay even with his powerful strokes and keep the prow of the boat headed toward the camp. We were soaked and my muscles ached when, with Ralph's help, we pulled the boat up on shore. But we were smiling at each other, and, above the roar of the wind and water, I heard the Major say, "It was a little exciting, but we made it."

When Mrs. Fleischmann met us in the yard, he said, "I have a great story to tell you."

He said to me, "Thanks, Buck, I enjoyed every minute of it."

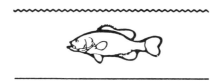

Nineteen forty-one was a busy year for the Major, and I find that my file contains seven letters from him, a letter and a telegram from Mrs. Fleischmann, and two letters from Mr. Julius Bergen.

On January 31, 1941, the Major wrote a long, newsy letter from his Hope Plantation in South Carolina, telling of his excellent fishing with light tackle for striped bass and his successful duck hunts. It also said, "I would have liked to stay a week or so longer, but owing to the fact that my ranchhouse in Nevada [Mason Valley] burned to the ground recently, I am beating it out West day after tomorrow and then communicating with David Vhay and Herb Dressler with the idea that I want to start rebuilding as soon as the weather clears."

In March he made a trip to Reno for a bank meeting and called me, and in April Mr. Bergen wrote that the Fleischmanns were on a trip to Mexico and Guatemala. I do not remember if we fished together in June, but a letter dated July 3 read,

Dear Buck:

Don't make any engagement for yourself for the week of August first or rather, the first week of August. If agreeable to you, I am going to take you on a fishing trip up in Oregon for a few days, where *Walt Whidden has promised us some three to four pounders or, he said, he would crawl on his hands and knees from Portland down here.* Will tell you all about it when I see you. Walt will be going with us, and I have all the data here.

All we will have to take are our sleeping bags and fishing rods, and we will have to pack in. We will have to drive about 390 miles from Reno, so it will mean an early start our first day, but we will take my car and take turns spelling one another.

Walter Whidden, for a number of years, was a very excellent executive for the Nevada Area Council of the Boy Scouts. He was highly respected by everyone interested in that youth organization, including Major Fleischmann. Eventually, he was promoted to a higher position in Oregon.

On July 23 Mr. Bergen wrote that the road we would be taking was in very bad condition, being under heavy construction, and that the automobile club advised that a trip over it was impracticable.

Apparently Walt telephoned the Major and arranged to meet him in Eugene. On July 25 I received a copy of a telegram from Major Fleischmann to Whidden: "Am arranging to land at Eugene between ten and eleven o'clock Friday morning August first. Confirm collect."

And so, on August first, when the Major's Lockheed airplane, with Captain Harry Ash and copilot Dan Withers at the controls, touched down at the Eugene airfield, Walt was waiting; and we were soon on our way to a lodge on Odell Lake. The two packers were ready for us, and before supper we turned over to them our tackle, sleeping bags, and the collapsible boat.

At the corral the next morning, one of the packers got me aside to ask about my riding experience, explaining that one of the best trail horses was somewhat temperamental. I told him that, in addition to horses, I probably had about a thousand miles on the back of a U.S. survey mule who liked nothing better than to try to knock me out of the saddle. I pointed out that Major Fleischmann was an excellent horseman, but the packer said that because of the Major's age, it was best to not take a chance on a broken bone. So I got the frisky one, and he turned out to be the best mountain horse I had ever ridden. He was almost as good as my mule.

It was a fifteen-mile ride with five saddle and two pack horses. I rode behind the Major and can still see him sitting straight, his shoulders square, as if he was on a military parade. After seven or eight miles he dismounted saying, "I'll give the horse a rest while I get some exercise." I followed his example but not for the same reason. It had been over a year since I had been in a saddle, and one part of my anatomy was getting a little sore.

We were in a thickly timbered forest of second-growth Douglas firs, and we soon reached an area of dead falls across the trail which several times caused a pack horse to go down. The second-growth trees were so close together that sunlight hardly touched the ground, and we noticed a stillness—a lack of bird songs—which we agreed was a little depressing.

But eventually we reached a more open area of mature Douglas firs where the bright colors of rhododendrons shown in the sun. Through the trees we soon glimpsed the lake, the Whidden paradise where four-pounders boiled the water when they started feeding.

With one eye on the water watching for a fish to rise, we set up camp. It was midafternoon when we put our fly rods together and headed for the shore where the Major was bending down to put his hand in the water. We saw the old master shake his head and mutter, "Warm surface water," and although we cast flies during the remainder of the afternoon and evening, we did not have a single rise.

A drizzling rain began the next morning, but, ignoring it, we began fishing the entire circumference of the lake. About noon I started wondering if some catastrophe—a poison or a lack of oxygen beneath the previous winter's ice—had destroyed the trout population. I had a spinning lure in my jacket and attached it to the leader in place of the fly. Casting it out into deep water, I let it sink to the bottom before retrieving it. On the second cast I had a strike and landed a twelve-inch rainbow. The Major was correct; the trout were not coming up into the warm surface water to feed.

If it was any consolation, that evening we did have an excellent dinner. During the morning the packers had dug a hole and built a fire in it which they allowed to burn down to a bed of coals. After covering the coals with a bed of rocks, they had placed a ham and several kinds of vegetables, wrapped in rhododendron leaves, on top of the rocks. The hole was then refilled with soil. In late afternoon when they again opened the pit, we could smell the ham across the lake. It was delicious.

That evening and the next morning, there was still no sign of feeding fish, so we broke camp and started for the lodge. Poor old Walt aged incredibly during those two days—on the way out his hunched shoulders were a pitiful sight. Three hundred and sixty miles by air, ninety miles by automobile, and fifteen miles by pack train, and not a single rise to a fly.

Actually, the Major and I were not unhappy with the trip. We had seen new country and enjoyed Walt's companionship. But we let him suffer for a few miles, mentioning how interesting it would be for tourists who would see a mature man crawling on his hands and knees down the highway to Reno. Eventually, we assured him that the water conditions were something he could not have anticipated and that, regardless of the fishing, we had enjoyed being with him.

Back at the lodge, a teen-age son of one of our packers was helping with our luggage. He had a bad case of facial pimples, and I was amused when the Major advised him to start taking Fleischmann's yeast.

The packers had admired the collapsible boat, which was ideally suited to their business. The Major gave it to them.

We stayed at a hotel in Eugene that night, and in the morning, on the way to the coffee shop, I stopped at the desk to pay for my room. The Major had already taken care of it, but he did let me pay for our breakfasts.

During our previous fishing trips we had shared the cost of transportation by alternating cars, and on the way to the airport I decided I should pay half the cost of the airplane's fuel. When I mentioned it to the Major, he said, "Absolutely no! This is my trip on my airplane, and you are not going to pay for one damn gallon of gas!" Later, I asked Captain Ash how much fuel the trip had taken and the price per gallon of aircraft gasoline. I do not remember the figures that he gave, but I do remember that a quick, approximate mental calculation brought the realization that I did not have enough money in my checking account to pay for half the fuel.

At the Reno airport, as we waited for transportation into town, we watched the airplane being serviced and stored in a hanger. It seemed that most of the airport personnel knew Major Fleischmann and several of them stopped by to say hello.

As we stood there, the Major turned to me and said, "You know, Buck, if I ever went broke I think there are people in Nevada who would grubstake me." I was surprised and pleased that he felt so warmly about Nevadans.

However, I wasn't too pleased with a later letter which ended with his typical dry humor, "I always enjoy being outdoors with you, but I would like to catch some fish occasionally."

I believe it was the weekend following our Oregon trip that the Major had an opportunity to judge my ability as a golfer.

On Sundays, Harold Curran, Clayton Phillips, Joe McDonnell, and I often played the Glenbrook golf course. Harold was the only proficient golfer of the foursome, but the rather fierce competition between the other three of us made the game enjoyable.

The three-par, third hole on the course was a wedge shot from tee to green, and as we approached it we saw Major Fleischmann waiting for us. He was taking his morning stroll and, noticing us on the second green, had decided to walk along for one or two holes.

Knowing the Major was an excellent golfer, I admit I was a bit nervous as I walked up to the third tee. For me a wedge had always been a difficult club, so while teeing up the ball I decided to play it safer and hit a soft nine iron.

A sand trap stretched across the front of the green; on the far side a grass-covered bank was supposed to protect the ball from a fifteen-foot drop to the sand and rocks of the lake's beach. Well, I did not hit the ball soft enough. It bounced across the green, rolled up and over the bank, and landed on the beach. I do not remember how I got on the green. Joe says I finally blasted it on for a double bogey.

Anyway, as we moved to the fourth tee, the Major said, "Buck, I think I'll walk another hole with you and maybe make a few comments." A lone fir tree graces the right side of the fourth fairway. I hit my drive, the ball drifted to the right, tucked itself away in the branches and needles of that tree— and remained there. When a second ball finally made it to the green, the Major came up to me and, with amusement in his eyes, said, "Buck, I think my only comment is, you could use a few more lessons." He then headed homeward.

Regarding Major Fleischmann and the game of golf, a story by Guy Shipler in *Nevada* magazine several years ago brought friendly smiles to many Nevadan faces. With the permission of Guy and editor-publisher Caroline Hadley, a few paragraphs of the article follows.

> The kids who caddied at the Glenbrook Golf Course at Lake Tahoe usually ducked out of sight when they saw the owner of the neighboring forty-four-acre estate coming to play a round. Each hoped that one of the other guys would be picked to carry his bag.

Not that they disliked the multimillionaire who lived a chip shot away from the course at a place he called "Upaway"; he was always polite and pleasant. And from a technical standpoint, Major Max C. Fleischmann was an ideal golfer. Unlike most of the regulars, he hit the ball straight. That kept caddies free from the dismal chore of trying to find balls hooked or sliced into the masses of stately but treacherous pines bordering Glenbrook's narrow fairways.

All the bag toters agreed that such precision was as fine a virtue as a player could have. It was just that even though Major Fleischmann was awfully rich, caddying for him was economically unsound. For like his famous golfing contemporary, John D. Rockefeller, Sr. (who had long since earned a world-wide notoriety for the same depressing habit), "The Major" usually tipped his caddy one thin dime after each round.

But not always. On a generous day, Fleischmann might go as high as a quarter.* "And sometimes," recalls one ex-caddy, "he would give us a candy bar instead. But in those days a candy bar cost only a nickel. So he actually got off for half price."

What puzzled the caddies was by then—some forty years ago—Major Max C. Fleischmann had acquired an unmatched reputation for philanthropy and good works. Already he had given away two million to institutions and charities in Nevada and millions more around the country before he became a resident of the state in the mid-thirties.[5]

Incidentally, the caddies Guy wrote about included my desert exploring companion, William "Bill" Bliss, who in later years was part owner of and managed the famous Glenbrook Inn; Robert "Bob" Laxalt, Nevada's widely respected writer; and United States Senator Paul Laxalt.

The Major would have enjoyed Guy's story.

---

*One of the former caddies stated that an average tip in those days was twenty-five cents. A one-dollar tip was very rare.

During the rest of the summer of 1941, the Major's interest in the Nevada State Museum occupied much of his time, and I was also quite busy. However, it was that year that I introduced the Major to the Carson River—a stretch of the stream south of Gardnerville known as the "Sheep Bridge." We used my Ford which had enough clearance to pass over the rocks of the steep and badly washed road which dropped down the side of the canyon to the river.

It was about midafternoon when we parked near the stream's bank, and I suggested that we hike upstream a mile or so and then fish back. The Carson River canyon, especially in late summer and fall, was well known for its rattlesnakes, and we had not walked far from the car when a buzzing sound, almost beneath our feet, made both of us jump. At the same instant we realized that our rattlesnake was a cicada.

For the next half mile or so, the ground was pockmarked with holes made by the larvae of these large insects as they tunneled to reach the surface after spending their allotted number of years (two to seventeen) underground. We watched them climb bush stems and then cling to a branch until their exoskeletons split open to free the enclosed winged adult which, when their wings became dry, were off to join the hundreds of their kind flying about. The noise they made drowned out the sounds of birds and the river. We both had witnessed this oddity of nature before, but it was still interesting.

The river was at a low stage, but from past experience I knew that the deep holes held large rainbow and brown trout which moved to the shallow riffles when the insect hatch began. We started using dry flies, and as the sun lowered behind the hills, fish began rising to them. There were no large ones landed that evening, but the ones we kept were the right size for the frying pan.

On the way home the Major mentioned that he was very impressed with the river and hoped we would make more trips to it.

In September the Fleischmanns left for Santa Barbara, and in early October I received an invitation to spend a weekend with them there. It was a long drive, but I appreciated their kindness and arranged with school officials to leave on a Friday morning. A letter from the Major provided directions to the Edgewood Ranch and outlined his plans for the visit.

I am tickled at the chance you will be down here next Friday. Now here is my schedule.

I have nothing on for Friday and nothing on Saturday so I will be glad to be at your disposal to play around here both days. My only suggestion is that you try to arrive here not later than Friday afternoon, coming out to Edgewood Ranch. We will have supper together and then take in the high school football game, Santa Barbara vs. San Diego. I am rather intimately connected with the local team.

You will stay over with us at Edgewood and, next morning, Saturday, we will go with plenty of time to putter around out at the Museum. You can either return Saturday or remain over for Sunday, when I am going down to my duck club, where we have an extra room, and you can see what my preserve is like, and start back Sunday. That you can settle when you are down here, but I am just telling you how I will be footloose.

I left Reno fairly early Friday morning but was delayed enroute, and on reaching a small town—I think about sixty miles from Edgewood—I realized I would arrive there later than they had planned. I stopped at a telephone booth and called their number.

An employee answered, and, after giving him my name and asking to speak to Major Fleischmann, he told me that the Major was ill and could not come to the phone. Before hanging up the receiver I made the decision that, with the Major ill, the visit would be an imposition on Mrs. Fleischmann, and that I should return to Reno. I gave the employee that message and started the long trip home. When I arrived in Reno, a telegram was waiting for me.

MAJOR MUCH BETTER. UP TODAY. TERRIBLY DISTRESSED. MISSED TALKING TO YOU MYSELF AND THAT YOU DID NOT COME ON DOWN HERE. PLEASE TRY AGAIN SOON. BEST RE-GARDS FROM BOTH OF US.

SARAH FLEISCHMANN

A letter arrived the next day which described the Major's illness and then added, "I was so sorry to be out walking the dog when you called up. The butler was a bit dumb not to find me. We were very disappointed that you did not get here—you were so near—but please let us know when you can really make it." The Fleischmanns were fine, gracious people, but I never found time to make a second trip to the Edgewood Ranch.

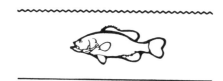

The year 1942 was one of frustration for both Major Fleischmann and me. The country was at war, but despite the Major's efforts, which included telephone calls to people in high places, his application for service had been turned down because of his age. Due to an old physical injury of mine which was not an actual handicap, two Selective Service examinations resulted in a 4F classification, and three attempts for a naval officer reserve commission and an application to the merchant marine were also unsuccessful. The Major gave his yacht *Haida* and his Lockheed airplane to the military.

Toward the end of that summer, we made a trip to the Carson River, and once again I did a stupid thing which turned out all right.

Arriving at the Sheep Bridge stretch of the river, we were putting our tackle together when I could not find my reel and line. I searched the car from one end to the other before remembering that I had taken it out of my fishing jacket to oil it and had not returned it. I told the Major I would watch him fish and still enjoy the trip. He said, "Absolutely not! we will take turns with my rod; it should be sort of interesting."

He was so definite that I knew there was no use arguing, so we hiked a mile or so up the stream to where we would start fishing back to the car. He handed me his beautiful little two-ounce, split bamboo Hardy rod, and told me to catch the first fish. The trout were hungry that evening, and on my second or third cast a fourteen-inch rainbow snatched my Royal Coachman and headed downstream. I was concerned about putting too much pressure on the light rod, and a second later the fish took to the air and the fly popped out of his jaw. The Major called, "You did not set the hook. What's wrong, are you getting weak in your old age?"

Well, that started the evening's routine, and we could not have had more fun.

I turned the Hardy over to him, and after several casts a brown trout, which must have weighed a good pound and a half, sucked in his fly and headed downstream in the swiftest part of the riffle. While giving it line, the Major tried to follow it from the bank, but a willow bush finally blocked his path and fouled his line. The fish broke the leader.

I called, "Why didn't you stay in the water away from those willows? Did you forget you were wearing waders?" He was smiling when he handed me the rod, but I could tell that he could hardly wait for me to lose another.

On the way upriver I had noticed a sort of weir stretching out into the river. There was a swift, deep run on the far side which spread out below into a shallower riffle. There were willows bending out over the water from the far bank, a good place for a large fish to be waiting for an insect to drop from the overhanging limbs. I waded out as far as possible, and with an extra cautious cast (I knew what would happen if I snagged a limb) I managed to shoot the line beneath the willows. The fly floated naturally with the current to where I was certain a fish would be lying, but there was no response.

After a half-dozen or so more casts (which, considering the snag hazard, I thought were nicely executed), I started back for the bank while slowly reeling in the line. Halfway back, the line still trailing downstream, I started to say something to the Major when a good-sized trout hit the fly. Attempting to turn toward the fish, I slipped on the algae-covered rocks and almost went down; while floundering about, my rod went parallel to the water just as the fish reached the end of the free line. Before I could release more line, and with no play in the rod, the hook came free.

I heard the Major laughing. He called, "That was the greatest exhibition of playing a fish I've ever seen. You're surely in great shape today." Well, we caught fish that evening, but I think we enjoyed the ribbing almost as much as the fishing.

We made one more enjoyable trip to the river that summer, and although I had my complete outfit with me, the Major insisted on the one-rod routine.

I believe it was in the fall of 1942 that the Major flew to Reno from Santa Barbara to be the main speaker at the Ducks Unlimited rally held in the University of Nevada gymnasium. Gene Shoupe was chairman of a committee which gathered prizes for a raffle, and Arthur Bartley, president of D.U., came out from New York to attend. The Major gave an excellent speech, and the raffle tickets raised over four thousand dollars toward the reclamation of waterfowl breeding marshes in Canada.

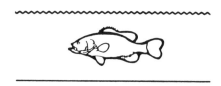

On March 15, 1943, Julius Bergen wrote to acknowledge a letter of mine written to the Major, who was hospitalized at the time.

As you know, he has not been feeling well off and on, and after returning from South Carolina last month he underwent a couple of thorough examinations. These disclosed nothing of a tumorous or malignant nature but did indicate the desirability of a certain type of operation. The first stage of this operation was performed last Friday to the satisfaction of Dr. Wills, and it will be completed day after tomorrow. It is not a pleasant ordeal, of course, but the doctor has no doubt of complete success, but it will mean hospitalization for several weeks. I am satisfied that the Major is in the best of hands.

Just as soon as he is able to take on a little business, I'll put your letter before him. He is always glad to hear from you.

One week later Mr. Bergen wrote,

Since writing you last week, the Major has been making satisfactory progress and considering his general ruggedness there can be little doubt as to a successful outcome. He is beginning to argue with doctor and nurse about this and that, which I would say was a favorable sign. I am sure he will soon be in a mood for reading and letters, at which time he will have your long, newsy letter, which he is bound to enjoy.

Toward the end of April, the Major sent a long letter which explained, "Your letters from Nevada were brought to me up at the hospital but I am frank to say I was so woozie at the time that it was only when I got back home again and could re-read them that I could grasp their contents." Explaining that he had undergone two surgeries within a period of a few days, he wrote, "so that alone gave me a terrific nervous shock which as yet I have not gotten over and doubt that I will get over it until I am able to get out and tramp, fish, and strengthen up my muscles."

When I returned to Nevada after spending the summer working at an Oakland shipyard, the Major and I made a trip to our secret lake. We almost wished we had not gone there, for where we parked the car we found cans, papers, other garbage, and human excrement scattered over the meadow grass. The Major was furious, and I thought of a name for the fishermen who had camped there. "Outdoor Slobs" described them so accurately that in future years I used it in lectures to my students. We dug a hole and buried the refuse. Apparently the lake had been heavily fished during the past two years. Only small brook trout rose to our flies.

During the summer of 1944 I worked in San Francisco as superintendent of a Red Cross warehouse. Clayton Phillips, who had been accepted by the Federal Bureau of Investigation, was stationed in the city, and I lived in a large apartment with him and two other FBI agents. It was quite an experience—such as the Sunday when Clayton and I went fishing for striped bass. He hooked a large ray which towed our small rowboat for an hour around the bay in a fog so dense we could not tell which way or where we were going. Finally we got the odd, flat-bodied fish alongside the boat where, after studying it for a few minutes, we released it.

I wrote the Major about our experience and received a return letter from him which noted, "Mrs. Fleischmann is doing a lot of Red Cross work so I will want to hear from you just where all this stuff has been shipped."

Upon my return to Reno for the school semester, the Major and I made a trip to Incline Lake. As we were waiting for the fish to start feeding, he was quiet and seemed to be thinking deeply. Suddenly he turned to me and said, "Buck, I think agriculture is Nevada's soundest business. More young people should go into it. It would benefit them and the state."

I wondered why he had been thinking about that subject; we had not discussed anything related to it. It was not until later in the year that I learned that he had given his 258-acre dairy farm (along with its dairy herd, equipment, and a

$150,000 endowment to aid in operational expenses) to the University of Nevada. In all of the years we fished together he never mentioned any of his gifts.

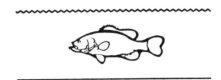

The winter of 1944 proved to be a time of decision. For many years, by state law, Nevada's seventeen county commissions had been charged with the primary responsibility of managing the state's fish and wildlife. The state fish and game commission, composed of five sportsmen from around the state, received only enough funds to support a fish hatchery and a secretary.

Because of many reports of poaching and a decline in fish and wildlife populations in many areas, a delegation of sportsmen met with Governor Carville to suggest that a director for the state commission be appointed who would meet with sportsmen in all of the counties and attempt to develop a unified effort to improve conditions. They suggested that I might be available for the position, and shortly thereafter, the chairman of the commission, Gene Phillips, offered me the job which would pay three thousand dollars a year.

I told him I would think about it, but if it meant leaving teaching permanently, I would not be interested. It was a difficult decision to make, so I wrote the Major for his advice. A part of his answer is an indication of the time and thought he was willing to spend on his friends.

When I got your letter I took it home, gave it considerable thought, and here are my conclusions.

Nevada has an unfortunate set of game laws and as long as the state has these game laws set up into counties, there will never be any effective legislation in that regard and there is bound to be political interference and favoritism. Therefore, anyone who would be able to change all this, put a uniform set of game laws in with proper enforcement, partly by paid and high-class game rangers and partly by sincere conservationists who would act as assistant game wardens and would have to take an oath of office so as not to be mere badge toters for effect—a great and constructive service would be done. HOWEVER, to carry this into effect would, I think, need an act by the state legislature and a legal opinion by the attorney general. Furthermore, any individual who would be considering trying to head a bureau such as this should do some very earnest sounding out of all the different game associations of the state to find out if they would be cooperative in this change.

Now, THEREFORE, as far as you are concerned, you would be a damn fool to take the position of director of fish and game for the State of Nevada unless:

(1) The legality of this were passed on by the attorney general and the legislature;

(2) You had a leave of absence of a year from next June, which would give you plenty of time to sound out the different game associations, etc., and that you step out of the picture and go back to your teaching job, which you are very fond of, in the event of this directorship not panning out;

(3) That in spite of the pay being good, $3,000 a year, there would be a liberal expense account attached thereto, for the simple reason that you will have to do an awful lot of chasing around the state by motorcar and all other means of travel reorganizing different counties into one state machine. You will have to personally interview and check up on your prospective game enforcement officers so that they are not political appointees and barroom bums.

Summed up then, I would say that if the attorney general rules on it properly, I think it is a job I think you would love. It ties right in with your biological work. It is outdoors—which you like—and it is constructive.

But you must have assurance that it is not a political appointment. It must be absolutely non-political, just like Judge Guild, who is a Republican and is head of the Nevada State Museum, and undoubtedly will be kept in by any succeeding administration as long as he does a good job.[6]

The Major's advice was sound, and he did realize that a change in the game laws of Nevada had to be initiated by the sportsmen of all counties in the state. Any attempt by the state commission would be received with suspicion and opposition, especially by the less populated counties where the best fishing and hunting areas were located. There were only a few really active sportsmen's organizations in the state, and the Major's suggestion of obtaining cooperation of sportsmen in every county had to be the first step.

I decided to meet with the state board and offer a compromise plan. The board was made up of well-known men: E. J. Phillips from Gardnerville, William "Al" Powell from Fallon, A. C. Barr from Ely, Fay L. Baker from Austin, and Leroy Cassidy from Austin. I explained to them that I did not wish to leave teaching but would be willing to work for them after school hours, on weekends, and during the summer. I asked that my salary be only fifty dollars a month to take care of extra travel expenses—those which state reimbursement did not cover. Finally, I suggested that instead of director, the job be titled representative of the state commission. My first project would be to attempt to establish an active sportsmen's organization in every county.

The board approved the plan, and when I wrote the Major about it, he decided it was a good way to start the program. So during the following months, armed with a set of bylaws general enough to temporarily fit any sportsmen's organization, I traveled the state.

In between my trips, the Major and I did manage to have several days of fishing together.

In May of 1945, at the fifty-fifth commencement exercises, the University of Nevada awarded Major Fleischmann an honorary Doctor of Laws degree. I remember sending him a congratulation card to which I added a footnote, "Do not expect me to address you as Doctor when we are out fishing."

During the summer months, I would now and then take a day off to go fishing with the Major. I think it was in 1945 that the Fleischmann's very close friends, Dr. and Mrs. J. A. Wiborn, came to Glenbrook for a visit. Dr. Wiborn was a widely known angler who, after retiring as chief eye surgeon at San Francisco's French Hospital, became a fishing companion of Zane Grey and Max Fleischmann. Made famous as the "Lone Angler" in Zane Grey's books, he was the first president of the Tyee Club of British Columbia and the only life member of the Catalina Tuna Club.[7]

The Major called to ask if I could take Dr. Wiborn and him to a stretch of the Carson River known as Youngs Crossing, which I had once mentioned as being good fly water. On picking them up at Glenbrook, I immediately liked Dr. Wiborn, a handsome elderly man, and as we drove, I listened to them reminisce about their trips to Alaskan, Canadian, and Mexican waters. At that time Dr. Wiborn held the record for the largest chinook salmon caught at the mouth of the Campbell River on Vancouver Island in British Columbia. I think it was while they were discussing it that I reverted to my childhood vocabulary and asked what size fishing "pole" he had used.

There was complete silence as both men turned to look at me, surprise on their faces. The Major asked the doctor, "Did you hear what I just heard?"

I knew what was wrong; it was a great sin to call a fishing rod a pole.

Doctor Wiborn said, "I thought a pole was something you hung telephone wires on."

Charles and Henriette Fleischmann. (Courtesy Julius Bergen)

Max, Charles, and Julius Fleischmann. (Courtesy Julius Bergen)

Early Cincinnati baseball team. Max Fleischmann, bottom row, second from left; Julius Fleischmann, middle, in white suit. (Courtesy Julius Bergen)

Max Fleischmann at graduation from Ohio Military Institute.
(Courtesy Julius Bergen)

First Lieutenant Max C. Fleischmann, left, with First Ohio Volunteer Cavalry, Spanish American War. (Courtesy Julius Bergen)

The auxiliary barkentine *Laura.*

The *Laura* anchors off the island of Skaarø for two days because of a heavy gale at sea.

A reindeer hunter's sod-covered hut on West Spitzbergen.

Butting ice plates caused a leak in the *Laura*'s bow which had to be repaired by ship's carpenters.

Fleischmann's photo of other members of his party on Jan Mayen
Island.

Remains of an Austrian expedition on Jan Mayen.

Provisions for bos'n and men who will spend the winter on Jan Mayen.

Sarah and Max Fleischmann ready to begin their safari.

The safari camp.

The world-famous photograph of a crocodile's attack on a rhinoceros.

Sarah Fleischmann and the baby antelope, M'Toto.

The record buffalo for British East Africa.

The safari heads back for Nairobi.

The Hudson Bay Company steamer, *Hazelton*, on the Stikine River.

Bob Reed and John Colbert throwing a diamond hitch.

Heading out.

Packing through broken timber.

Camp work.

Skinning out the record stone sheep head.

Caribou country.

The cache of trophies.

The war canoe built by the Haida Indians, which will take Fleischmann and Little downriver to Wrangell.

Fleischmann was impressed with the skill of the five Indian crew members.

The motor launch *Taku.*

Eliza Harbor.

Fleischmann, Little, and Captain Lancaster relaxing in the sun.

The Trophy Hall, which was used as a library. (Courtesy Santa Barbara Museum of Natural History)

The widely known exhibit in the Sarah Hamilton Fleischmann Bird Hall. (Courtesy Santa Barbara Museum of Natural History)

En route to the Lagna River, bullock carts replaced automobiles to carry supplies into the jungle. (Fleischmann-Clark Indo-China Expedition. Courtesy Dept. Library Services, American Museum of Natural History)

The United States Mint at Carson City in the 1870s. (Courtesy Nevada State Museum)

That grand old Nevadan, Judge Clark J. Guild. (Courtesy Nevada State Museum)

Mannequin operating drill in the mine. (Courtesy Nevada State Museum)

Red Lake below Carson Pass. (Courtesy Harold Curran)

The east fork of the Carson River. (Courtesy Nevada State Department of Wildlife)

Aftermath of Fishing Trip

Scheduled to be run last week, but delayed through technical difficulties, the above sketch is designed to illustrate Sessions Wheeler and Major Max C. Fleischmann exacting the payment promised them by Walter Whidden for the party's failure to return from an Oregon packing trip laden with trout. Whidden, guide on the journey, offered to crawl from Portland to Reno if the fishing wasn't superb. No other mention except the illustration need be made concerning the trip, Wheeler asserts.

Sketch attached to the weekly newspaper column written by the author and William O. Bay. (Courtesy *Reno Evening Gazette*)

Dr. J. A. Wiborn. His 63½-pound salmon (a record for the Tyee Club) is not the one in the photograph.

The game farm near Verdi that was largely built from ammunition boxes and other salvaged materials. (From motion picture filmed by author for Nevada State Fish and Game Commission)

The flag of the USS *Nevada* being presented to the state of Nevada. Major Fleischmann, far left; Governor Vail Pittman, third from left. The event occurred before the Fleischmann-Pittman confrontation. (Courtesy Nevada State Museum)

Smith Valley rearing station. (From motion picture filmed by author for Nevada State Fish and Game Commission)

Murl Emery's floating dock on the Colorado River. (From motion picture filmed by author for Nevada State Fish and Game Commission)

The big ram walked out on a ridge above us. (From motion picture filmed by author for Nevada State Fish and Game Commission)

Heavy earth-moving equipment given to Ducks Unlimited Canada by Major Fleischmann. The Cat tractor was named "The Major" by D.U. personnel. (Courtesy Ducks Unlimited)

Major Fleischmann and the famous Jimmy Robinson at Hope Plantation. (Courtesy Jimmy Robinson)

Jimmy Robinson's photograph of the Major during their quail hunt at Hope Plantation. This is the author's favorite picture of the Major. (Courtesy Jimmy Robinson)

Morley "Bill" Griswold and his father, former Nevada governor Morley Griswold, ready to leave for their trip on the *Haida*. (Courtesy Bill Griswold)

The Major fighting a marlin. (Courtesy Julius Bergen)

Food aboard the *Haida* was delicious.

MENU
****

SPECIAL CLAM CHOWDER

*****

ROAST YOUNG TURKEY GIBLET SAUCE

BRUSSEL SPROUTS   CRANBERRY SAUCE

****

FRESH RASPBERRY SUNDAE

BREAKFAST - SUGGESTIONS
****

BOILED EGGS
SCRAMBLED EGGS AND BACON
SHIRRED EGGS AND BACON
EGGS BEURRE NOIRE
BUCKWHEAT CAKES,SYRUP
HAM AND EGGS
SPANISH OMELET
WAFFLES AND HAM
SMOKED ALASKA COD
CREAMED FINNAN HADDIE
KIPPERED HERRING
TRIPE CREOLE

The salon. (From *America's Outstanding Seagoing Diesel Yacht, Haida*)

The dining room. (From *America's Outstanding Seagoing Diesel Yacht, Haida*)

The *Haida.* (From *America's Outstanding Seagoing Diesel Yacht, Haida*)

Nevada Wheeler fighting coho.

The Major, with guide Jack Lowry rowing, hooks a coho.

Captain Dave Welch as the *Haida* enters Ketchikan harbor.

Nevada and Jack Lowry in front of Ketchikan post office.

Admiralty Island fly fishing.

The *Haida Papoose* heads for Stewart Edward White's trail.

I couldn't think of anything to say, so I just nodded, smiled, and kept quiet.

When we reached the river, I guided them to the best riffles. Dr. Wiborn, like the Major, was an expert with a fly rod, and they both caught fish.

At the end of the day, while walking back to the car, I saw the Major wink at Dr. Wiborn and heard him say something like, "I just don't know how Buck can cast that line with a telephone pole."

That was the last time I ever called a fishing rod a pole.

In 1945 the Major replaced the airplane that he had turned over to the military in 1942. The cabin of the new plane, a Lockheed Lodestar, was modified with a decrease in the number of regulation passenger seats to allow space for several upholstered chairs and a davenport which could be converted to a bed. On some trips, when an early takeoff was planned, the Major would sleep on his airplane, which he named the *Silver Falcon*.

That fall, with the cooperation of Churchill County sportsmen, the Nevada State Fish and Game Commission undertook one of its most important and long-lasting projects. The great Stillwater marsh, northeast of Fallon, had provided a significant waterfowl breeding area, as well as a hunting ground, from the time of the prehistoric Indian to the present. Since the days of Nevada's pioneers, it had been open to hunting free of charge.

Fallon sportsmen became aware of a rumor that a group of wealthy out-of-state men were planning to attempt to lease exclusive hunting rights on the marsh. When the fish and game commission was notified, negotiations to save the area were given priority over all other projects.

The Truckee-Carson Irrigation District, under its agreement with the U.S. Bureau of Reclamation, controlled the area. After a series of meetings between its board of directors, the state commission, and Churchill County sportsmen, the commission obtained a lease which guaranteed free public use for a period of five years. Under Bureau of Reclamation regulations, a lease of more than five years could not be approved unless another federal agency was involved.

During the next four years, negotiations with the U.S. Fish and Wildlife Service finally resulted in a new fifty-year agreement which, while allowing a relatively small section of the marsh to become a refuge, established one of the largest free public hunting areas in the country. Empowered by the fish and game commission, I signed the agreement on November 26, 1949.

The Major had followed every step of the project and was pleased with the outcome. Knowing that the great marsh was an important resting area for migrating waterfowl and shore birds and a nesting area for local ducks, geese, swans, shore birds, and other wildlife, he favored the protection offered by the refuge and believed that the remainder of the marsh should be open to all sportsmen rather than a relatively few who could afford belonging to a private club.

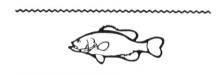

The Major was intensely interested in everything we were doing for Nevada wildlife. I attempted to keep him informed, but he apparently was obtaining information from other sources. On February 11, 1946, a letter from the Major included,

Was a little disturbed when I heard about the fire in the Lyons Building [in downtown Reno], thinking a lot of your records might have been destroyed, but since heard that you are established at the University of Nevada somewhere, so since you do not mention anything to the contrary I imagine everything is going along O.K.

By the beginning of that year, the state fish and game commission had found enough money for me to hire Shirl Coleman, a young graduate in wildlife management from Utah State University, who would work both as a state warden and technician. We had an office in the old Lyons Building and one secretary, Adeline Benner.

It was late in January that my secretary called me at school to tell me that the Lyons Building was on fire. I left my class on the run, told the principal to get a free teacher or someone to take my class, and broke a few traffic laws. Flames were erupting from the roof of the building.

Knowing Adeline, I was sure she was trying to save the files, and dodging a fireman who was yelling, "You can't go in!" I ran up the stairs to our second-floor office where I found her calmly removing the files from the cabinets. I told her to get outside, but she said, "I certainly will not, I'm going to help you get the files." I had learned from experience that there was no use arguing with her, and in four or five trips, our files and typewriter were outside on the sidewalk. A small bar across the street allowed us to store them in a back room.

We had to have a new office immediately, and the rent had to be cheap. I remembered a small empty room at the university's zoology laboratory, and called my old friend and major professor, Dr. Phillip Lehenbauer. He arranged for us to move in, and we stayed there, rent free, for about the next two years.

On May 9, the Major wrote in part,

> I was up in Nevada for a week . . . busy as a bird dog at the ranch. . . . I went out to the university as I heard that was your headquarters, but your office told me you were not in. Sorry to have missed you.
>
> There appears to be quite a lot of activity at the old people's home on your fish tanks, and I saw people working there on my way out to the ranch.

The holding tanks the Major referred to were built next to the county home located near the intersection of U.S. highways 395 and 50 en route to Lake Tahoe. The fish were fed by the elderly people prior to being transplanted to various streams. The tanks were constructed by fish and game people and members of the Ormsby County Sportmen's Association—one example of the excellent cooperation the new program was receiving. Throughout the state, with sportsmen's organizations so eager to be of aid, the program was developing into a sort of wildlife improvement crusade. This impressed the Major—he expressed admiration for the Nevadans who were donating their time and efforts to this conservation movement.

The commission and the sportsmen were beginning to think about trying to improve upland game bird populations, and about that time I met Charles A. "Hap" Early, a retired superintendent of transportation and equipment for the city of Los Angeles. Early in World War II, during the training of General Patton's Third Army in the Mohave Desert, he was called upon to act as Patton's administrative assistant because of his knowledge of transportation and heavy equipment. The general wanted to get him a commission in the army, but Hap turned it down, saying there would be too much red tape.

Hap, a big man with a brilliant mind, was a brother-in-law of our secretary, and one day he came to the office to see her. While he was there, I mentioned our need for a game farm and told him that we had the land for it in the vicinity of the state fish hatchery (near Verdi) but did not have the money to build it. Hap had retired with a pension, so time and salary were of no concern to him. Apparently insoluble problems had always captured his interest. A day or so later he called to ask if I wanted some help in finding a way to build the farm.

I talked it over with the commissioners, and they found enough money in the budget to pay a salary that would have insulted any other fish and game employee in the country. It was fine with Hap, though, and he went to work to find free materials to build a brooder house, pens, runways, etc. There was an ancient barn on the property, and he soon had braced its walls, repaired the roof, painted it red with white trim, and converted it to a workroom where he could use his large personal collection of power and hand tools. The Major spent some time with Hap and felt that he was just the type of man we needed.

By this time, a number of the sportsmen's clubs were helping our state hatchery plant fish and build holding ponds and were providing aid in other projects. Most of the members of the Mineral County Sportsmen's Association were employees of the large naval ammunition depot at the south end of Walker Lake; with the war ended, Hap thought there might be surplus material at the depot that we could use. So we headed for Hawthorne to meet with Allen Conelly, an active member of the county organization.

Conelly said that there were hundreds of strongly built wooden ammunition boxes about four feet long and eight inches in depth and width which, fastened together, would make strong, insulated walls. Also there were innumerable steel rocket tubes about four feet long which could be welded together for fence posts. He said that if we could find transportation, members of the sportsmen's association would load the boxes and tubes.

One of the routes of Wells Cargo, Inc. ran through Hawthorne. Brothers Bob and Joe Wells were sportsmen, and they readily agreed to take on a load, free of charge, each time one of their large, empty trucks was returning to Reno. Hap borrowed a cement mixer, and with the help of his brother-in-law, Gus Benner, and Hap's son, Ray, (fresh out of the navy), he had the foundation for the brooder house in place when the boxes began arriving. Working ten to twelve hours a day for seven days a week, the building went up fast, and Hap, with his own welding equipment and used chicken wire, soon had some of the runways built. Now all that we needed were brood birds.

About that time (July 1946) there was a conference in Twin Falls, Idaho, of the fish and game directors and commissioners of the eleven western states. With the hope of obtaining brood stock from one of the other states, I decided to attend; the Major, who had been following the progress of the game farm with great interest, said he would like to accompany me. The Major attended both the general and technical meetings on subjects in which he was interested and spent the remainder of his time walking the streets of the city viewing merchandise. On several of our trips I learned that he was an inveterate "window-shopper."

Following one of the afternoon sessions of the conference, the Major and I were invited to fish a private lake in the Snake River canyon. We were told that it was filled with very large rainbow trout, so we were eager to try it—and even visited a local sporting goods store to buy some larger flies than the ones we had with us.

After driving on a road cut into the perpendicular rock walls of the deep canyon, we found that the small lake was fed by a large spring. The water was so clear that we could see rainbow trout weighing at least four to five pounds cruising along the bottom.

We got our rods together quickly and started casting the large flies. Neither of us had a strike, so we changed to the smaller imitation insects. We worked entirely around the shore of the lake; not a single one of the large trout was interested enough to swim up and look at what we offered.

Finally, the caretaker stopped by to see how we were doing. When he saw our tackle, he shook his head and said, "You won't catch them on flies in this lake. Since we introduced freshwater crayfish, that's about all they eat. I can loan you some tackle and bait if you want to catch fish." We thanked him but turned down his offer and headed for town.

Several of the states having game farms offered to provide pheasant brood stock, so, as the Major said, "The trip was a success. You got the birds you needed, and, although we didn't catch a fish, we saw some new country."

In November a letter from the Major mentioned, "I am very much interested in the Annual Report of your fish and game program and really think you are making as much progress as possible."

During 1946 and early 1947, representatives of county sportsmen's associations worked together to develop a new fish and game management plan for Nevada. When the 1947 legislature began its session, they proposed a bill which would establish a restructured Nevada State Fish and Game Commission of seventeen members—one member from each county. The act also provided that each county would have a Game Management Board of three sportsmen who would have considerable power to manage the wildlife resources of their county. All income from the sale of licenses or other sources would be placed in the state treasury to the credit of the State Fish and Game Fund. County boards would prepare budgets, and the state commission would have the responsibility of allocating funds for both county and state projects. Largely due to the efforts of State Senator Warren Monroe of Elko County and the sportsmen's clubs throughout the state, the act was passed by the state legislature and went into effect on July 1, 1947.

At their first meeting, the new commission asked me to take a year's leave of absence from my teaching position to serve as the commission's director. I wished to return to teaching, and I knew the Major was concerned about possible political problems. But during the past two years, most or all of those seventeen men had worked with me, and when they put it on the basis of helping them get the program started, I could not refuse. The next day's local newspaper pointed out, "Wheeler accepted the post at the urging of . . . the commission and only after he had emphasized he intended to 'stay with the job just long enough to help get the new system underway.'"[8] After reading the newspaper article, Major Fleischmann decided I had made the only reasonable decision.

There was so much to be done during the remainder of 1947 that it could not have been accomplished without the help of county sportsmen. One project was the construction of a new cutthroat-trout rearing station in Smith Valley; sportsmen turned out to help state employees dig ditches, lay pipe, and pour cement. State Highway Engineer Larry Chambers of the Ormsby County sportsmen's club provided all of our engineering needs.

Nine new state game wardens were hired and trained with the help of a U.S. Fish and Wildlife Service agent, C. J. Fairchild. Fisheries biologist Thomas Trelease was developing an inventory and stocking program for all suitable waters in the state, and two competent big-game biologists were employed to help manage deer herds.

In earlier years chukar partridge had been established in Nye County largely through the efforts of two fine members of the Nye County sportsmen's club, Walter Bowler and Thomas McCulloch. In one area the birds were reaching an overpopulation which could result in disease. The state hired an experienced man, Harold Peer of Fallon, to trap and distribute some of the chukars to other parts of the state. Over one thousand wild birds were redistributed, starting populations where they had not before existed.

I only had time for one fishing trip with the Major that year, but we kept in touch. One evening I dined with the Fleischmanns at their Glenbrook home and found a gift at my place at the table. Mrs. Fleischmann knew that I liked wool socks, and she had knitted several pairs for me.

In December 1947 a letter from the Major made me wonder if his interest in our upland game bird program had started him thinking about doing something similar on land surrounding his Old Adobe duck club. He wrote,

> I am going right ahead with my plans to turn the Old Adobe into a game management non-commercial place. I have ordered eight breeding pairs of pheasant which are due to arrive in January and I am going to put their eggs out under Silkies or Bantams, probably the former. This is experimental. . . . I am also going to plant quite a bit of corn for feed.

The Major returned to Nevada from Hope Plantation early in 1948, moving into his Jacks Valley Ranch home in February. One day in March he stopped at the office just as I was about to leave for the fish hatchery, and I invited him to come along. The Verdi hatchery was in full operation, and Superintendent Les Nicholas and Sebastian Coli showed us some new rearing ponds under construction. They also took us through the hatchery building where the Major was particularly interested in the care of the eggs and tiny fry.

On the return to Reno I decided to tell him about a personal matter—Miss Nevada Pedroli and I planned to be married in April. Both he and Mrs. Fleischmann had met and liked her.

He seemed very pleased and, after offering congratulations, asked, "Will she continue to teach?"

I said that she loved teaching and would stay with it indefinitely.

I clearly remember what he then said, "That's excellent, Buck. Now you will have two salaries coming in and should be able to build up your savings." The Major was a practical man.

In May of 1948, the Major got angry—very angry—at the governor of the State of Nevada.

Back in 1936, Governor Kirman had appointed the Major a reserve member of the Nevada State Police, and in 1942 Governor Carville had renewed the appointment.

The highway between Glenbrook and Zepher Cove had only two lanes with several curves that were dangerous for anyone exceeding the speed limit. Because of several bad accidents, the Major, although unpaid, decided to attempt to make the highway safer. With a siren and flashing red light installed on his car and a Nevada State Police insignia painted on each side, he started patrolling the highway.

Undoubtedly his army experience, along with his reasonableness, made him a good officer. Several drivers whom he stopped told me that he was very polite as he explained why speed was dangerous to both them and to others along the curving road. If their speed was far enough above the limit to be considered reckless, they were given a citation. Otherwise, they received a warning. His patrol had a marked effect on reducing accidents.

I remember that, at least once, he was assigned to take part in a search for an escaped convict from the state prison.

When Lester Moody, who had been a peace officer in Nevada for many years, became superintendent of the Nevada State Police, he and the Major became good friends. And so, on May 20, 1948, when Governor Vail Pittman demanded Lester Moody's resignation, the Major headed for the governor's office.

I remember the rumors that followed the meeting—that it was a heated confrontation with both men yelling at each other. One source said that it almost developed into fisticuffs. Some days later, Lester Moody was dismissed after refusing to resign, and a thoroughly disgusted Major Fleischmann left the law enforcement agency, turning in his badge and gun and removing the state police insignia from his car. Later in the year he accepted an appointment as U.S. Deputy Marshal for the District of Nevada.

During the summer, when possible, I would take a day during a weekend to fish with the Major. One Saturday afternoon we drove to a stretch of the Carson River named Horseshoe Bend which in the 1930s had been known for large rainbow and brown trout. My fly box still contained five of the large grey-hackle, peacock-body flies used for big fish in those days.

During the afternoon we fished downstream keeping in sight of each other, but as evening settled in we became separated. Not knowing whether the Major was above or below me, I decided to wait for him at my favorite riffle not far from the car.

The riffle was long and swift, flowing into a deep hole beneath an overhanging cliff, and I remembered that an underwater ridge of hard rock, jutting out from the eroded cliff, had been a hazard to a taut line. Replacing a small dry fly with one of the large grey hackles, I waded into the river about thirty yards above the hole and cast upstream. The fly had floated less than twenty feet when there was a savage strike and a rainbow, which I judged to be close to seven pounds, lashed itself almost clear of the surface and then headed downstream.

The line was shooting from the reel, cutting the water toward the cliff, as I attempted to reach the shore to follow the fish and obtain a better angle to turn it away from the ridge. But there was not time—the big rainbow reached the hole, there was a violent lunge, and the leader snapped.

It was difficult to believe, but during the next half hour I lost all but one of the large flies in almost the same way. I was tying on the last grey hackle when I suddenly realized that the leader was the same 5x (two-pound test) one I had used with dry flies during the afternoon. Saying some unkind words to myself, I changed to a heavier leader.

Every two or three minutes I had been calling for the Major, hoping to get him on the riffle, but it was getting near the daily closing time, and I was starting to wade into the stream when I heard him call. He had landed several fish but no large ones. I quickly explained what had been happening and said, "My rod and leader are heavier than yours, and I want you to tie into one of those giants." He started to protest; I told him we did not have time to argue, and he reluctantly took my rod and waded into the stream.

On his second cast he had a heavy strike, and the line started downstream. The Major quickly backed out to the bank and started following the fish. I called to him, "If it gets to the hole keep it away from that cliff."

He was putting pressure on the rod and maintaining an

angle that was forcing the trout toward the center of the river, away from the rock ridge. Fifteen minutes later, near the lower end of the hole, he slid a beautiful five-pound brown trout onto the sandy shore.

The legal fishing day was over, and we took the rods down. On the way back to the car we decided to tie a handful of large grey hackles and fish Horseshoe Bend again. Two weeks later we were on the riffle, and although it was not as fast and furious as before, with proper tackle we landed several nice fish.

A school board regulation limited a leave-of-absence to one year, but at the annual fish and game commission meeting in July 1948, the commissioners passed a resolution requesting a "loan" of the teacher for another year. There were several projects I wanted to finish, so when the school board agreed to the request, I stayed with the job.

During August I was making weekly day trips to the rearing pond in Smith Valley where we were attempting to rear cutthroat trout. One day I stopped by the Jacks Valley Ranch to pick up the Major who wished to ride out with me to see the new station.

On previous trips I had seen something of interest to a naturalist. Each day, shortly beyond where the road branches from Highway 395 to Smith Valley, I had seen a small cottontail rabbit which was always sitting in the same place, apparently watching the cars go by. As we drove along I told the Major about it and he asked, "Did you say it was exactly in the same place every time?"

His voice was skeptical, and I answered, "Yes! Every time."

We were getting near the rabbit's area and I thought to myself, "This will probably be the only day that darn cottontail will not be there, and I'll never live down my wild story."

As we reached the turnoff, the Major said, "Well, let's see your crazy rabbit."

I answered halfheartedly, wishing I hadn't mentioned the whole thing, "He should be on the other side of the road just behind that bush where the road bends."

And there, in exactly the same place, was sitting that reliable little car-watcher. I breathed an inaudible sigh of relief as the Major said, "If I hadn't seen it, I would have had difficulty believing it."

In Smith Valley, in addition to visiting the rearing station, we watched early flights of sprig (pintail) ducks circle and glide on set wings down to a flooded field. Altogether it was an enjoyable day.

In early September Earl Branson, our state fish and game commissioner from Ormsby County, invited the Major and me to fish with him at Youngs Crossing where he had recently enjoyed good fishing. Using Earl's truck, we took a shorter but somewhat more dangerous route to the river than I had used on the previous trip with Dr. Wiborn. The road down into the canyon was narrow and slanted sideways enough to cause the Major and I to stand on the high-side running board to keep the car from tipping and possibly sliding down the hillside. On one especially bad stretch, I glanced at the Major. He was smiling, and I could see that he was enjoying this small adventure.

We caught fish, but it was one of my absent-minded days. I had forgotten to bring along a supply of my favorite fly for afternoon fishing, and I called to the Major to see if he had an extra one.

He tossed me his small aluminum dry-fly box, a new type with which he was very pleased. It differed from the common container by using magnetized bars instead of clasps to hold the flies in place. At the moment it was his most valued piece of equipment although it had cost about one dollar.

I found the fly I needed, and rather than take the chance of tossing the box back to him while he was in water up to his waist, I stuffed it into the back pocket of my Levis.

On the way home we stopped at a restaurant for dinner, and when we left, and were several miles down the road, I remembered that I had left my hat on the coat rack. Turning back to retrieve it, I heard the Major say, "Earl, I think Buck is becoming a typical absent-minded professor."

We drove the Major up to his Glenbrook home and had started to leave when I had a feeling that I had forgotten something. I asked Earl to stop for a moment and then saw the Major hurrying toward us. He said, "Glad you remembered my new fly box."

I dug into my back and front Levi pockets, my shirt and fishing jacket pockets—I did not have it. We searched the car without success, and I decided it must have popped out of my back pocket somewhere along the stream. The Major said, "Don't worry about it; I'll send for another one." But I knew I had lost something that he prized.

The next morning I went to one of Reno's sporting goods stores hoping, but not really expecting, to find one of the newly designed boxes. The store had recently received a shipment, and that evening I took one up to the Major. When he opened the package, I could see his gratitude.*

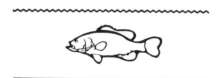

During the spring of 1949, the Major and I had an exceptionally interesting trip. I had wanted him to see and fish the Colorado River, and partly because he had paid the expenses of the Oregon pack trip, I wrote him that on this one he would be my guest.

I suggested that he fly from Santa Barbara to Las Vegas where we would meet. He agreed and said that following our trip he had business in Reno and, if I could get to Las Vegas without my car, I could fly back with him.

---

*Several years after the death of the Major, Earl removed the front seat of his truck for cleaning. The Major's box was underneath; it had slipped between the seat and its back. I told Earl to keep the box and its flies.

It so happened that my assistant director, Frank Groves, was scheduled to spend two days at Nelson Landing, a fishing camp on the river where the Major and I would stay. We decided to drive down the day before the Major would arrive to take care of some business in Las Vegas.

The Major arrived fairly early in the morning, and Frank drove us to Nelson Landing which was operated by Murl Emery, one of the best-known fishing guides in the West.

Murl had several guest cabins, a small restaurant, and a large barge anchored to the bank of the river on which he had built his shop for repairing and storing outboard motors, selling fishing tackle, etc. On the downstream end, his rental boats were tied to the barge, and there was deck space with easy chairs where anglers could relax and tell their stories about the big ones that broke their leaders.

The stored water from the recently completed Davis Dam had backed up the river to within a short distance of the landing, but upstream, where we would fish, the river had not yet been affected.

I had known Murl since the state had begun planting large numbers of fingerling rainbow trout in the river. Probably everyone who knew him considered him an especially interesting character—a big man with a dry sense of humor who, according to the circumstances, could be a typical old-time riverman or a well-educated gentleman. I knew the Major would enjoy him.

On arriving at the river, Murl told us that he had two boats ready, and as soon as we had stored our bags in one of the cabins and put our tackle together, we would take off with him and his son as guides. Frank and I went with his son, and I asked Murl to take the Major in his boat and show him some of the remnants of the old days when riverboats, powered by steam, fought their way upstream against strong currents and through rapids. I had traveled the river many times with Murl and with our southern Nevada game warden, Steve Fenton, who had pointed out the ring bolts anchored in giant boulders to which steamers had attached their winch ropes to help pull them through the heaviest water.

The fishing boats were equipped with large outboard motors, and we sped upriver through beautiful Eldorado Canyon for approximately ten miles before turning back to fish and drift slowly downstream, dropping anchor in the best areas. The rainbows were fat and strong, and when we worked them to the side of the boat, they were released.

We were about halfway back to camp when Murl, pointing towards shore, motioned us to follow him. We saw that several desert bighorn sheep were feeding near the river, but as we approached they withdrew up a draw in the canyon wall. We sat quietly in our boats hoping they would reappear. Suddenly a big ram, with an especially large curl of horns, walked out on a ridge above us. He seemed unafraid—the hunting of bighorn sheep had not been legal along the Colorado for many years—and we had the opportunity to study the marvelous creature. The Major did not take his eyes from it, and when we again started downstream, I saw that he had turned to watch the animal until we rounded a bend and it was lost from sight. He later told me that seeing that ram was worth the trip.

We had dinner that evening at the little restaurant, and when the waitress placed the check on the counter the Major started to reach for it, but I quickly took it.

He said, "Buck, let me take care of the expenses."

I answered in a very definite tone of voice, "Major, I told you that this is my trip, and that is the way it is going to be! Nevada and I have budgeted all of it."

He hesitated for a moment and then asked, "You mean that you have it in your monthly budget?"

I answered, "Absolutely."

"Well," he smiled, "I guess it's all right then."

Apparently, the Major had great respect for a budget.

Following dinner we walked down to Murl's barge where several other fishermen were relaxing. With the heat of the day cooled to a pleasant temperature and the sound of the river gently slapping against the sides of the barge, it was a pleasant atmosphere for sitting and talking.

Murl, who must have known something about the Major's hunting and fishing expeditions, began requesting information about certain places in Alaskan and Mexican waters. Surprisingly to me, the Major talked freely about his twenty-one Alaskan trips and his marlin fishing in southern waters. Murl had the ability to keep the Major reminiscing, and I am certain everyone found the conversation intensely interesting.

Eventually we decided to get some sleep. Our cabin had bunk beds, and the Major insisted on sleeping on one of the top ones. I can still see him climbing up to his bed, wearing what appeared to be long underwear. During the night I awakened several times to hear him tossing. Frank says he clearly remembers that in the morning, the Major was the first out of bed, calling, "Everybody up—there's no pleasure without pain." Later he admitted that he had not slept very soundly.

We fished for several hours that morning, and after lunch Frank was ready to drive us back to Las Vegas. I left the Major packing his gear and went to the barge to settle my bill with Murl. I knew that anglers paid a premium price for his services, and I had brought along my checkbook.

I asked Murl what I owed him. He answered, "Not one cent."

I said, "Listen, Murl, I know about what you charge, and I'm going to write a check for it."

He said, "Go ahead, but it will be wasted effort because I'll tear it up."

I started to ask why he wasn't charging me, but he interrupted to say, "Major Fleischmann is doing much for this state and you have helped this river."

I said, "The commission planted the fish in the river."

I guess he was tired of arguing; he said, "Listen, Buck, this is my place, my boats, my cabins, and my guide service. I can charge any damn amount I want to charge. In this case the charge is zero. If you want to sue, get a lawyer."

I knew further argument was useless so I thanked him. I did manage to tip his son when Murl was not around.

On the way back to Las Vegas I told the Major, "Murl would not accpet payment because of what you had done for Nevada." I could see that he was surprised and grateful, but he did not say anything. Frank, who would continue on to Tonopah, dropped us off at the Thunderbird Hotel where we had reserved rooms. In the lobby the Major asked, "Buck, will you do me a favor?"

I nodded, and he said, "You've taken me on a very enjoyable trip, but now the trip is over, and we are back in civilization. I want you to invite any friend or friends you have here in Las Vegas to come out to the hotel for dinner. And I want to pay the bill."

Because of the way he asked, it would have been ungracious to not accept; so I thanked him and said, "I would like to invite our state fish and game commissioner from Clark County. I know Cal Liles would enjoy meeting you."

The three of us had an excellent dinner and afterwards moved outside to relax in lawn chairs beside the swimming pool. Like the previous evening, the weather was balmy, and the Major was again in a talkative mood. With Cal urging him on with questions, he related anecdotes and impressions of Teddy Roosevelt, Bernard Baruch (who had a plantation near the Major's in South Carolina), and his many other famous American friends. It was fascinating, and I have often wished that somehow it had been recorded.

Around eleven o'clock I began worrying about the Major's lack of sleep the preceding night, and I suggested that we call it an evening. Cal rose and thanked the Major and left. I thought the Major looked tired when we parted in the lobby.

The next morning when I paid the cashier for my room, I learned that the Major had already checked out. I knew the hotel's security man, and when I met him in the lobby he said that the Major had taken a short walk. He added, "When Major Fleischmann tried to pay his room bill, the management would not accept his money, saying it was their way of expressing gratitude for his aid to the university and other Nevada organizations."

The Major seemed to be rested and in a happy mood when we took a taxi and started for the airport. But about halfway there, he suddenly turned to me and said, "Damn it, Buck, why did you break it up so early last evening? I was having a hell of a good time."

Attempting to keep from smiling, I said, "We didn't get much sleep the night before."

We had a pleasant trip to Reno in the *Silver Falcon*, and as we parted at the airport he said, "Buck, it was a great trip."

CHAPTER FOUR

The Last Years (1950 – 1951)

In the mid 1940s, the Major had built a small lake (actually a pond) on his Jacks Valley Ranch, and when I stopped to see him shortly after he arrived in the spring of 1950, he asked if I knew where he could buy some eight- to ten-inch rainbow trout. I told him there was a commercial trout farm south of Reno, and offered to contact the owner, Bill Mulheron. Bill, a fine person, said that he would be glad to take a load of fish out to the ranch. I did not discuss price—that would be up to the Major.

About a month later, I stopped by the ranch. The Major had a light rod and line with a barbless hook already set up, and we walked down to the pond. On his second cast a rainbow grabbed his fly, and after playing it for a minute or so, the Major very carefully released it. He was delighted with his pond, and on the way back to the house he told me that Bill Mulheron had refused to accept payment for the fish.

By this time, the Major must have realized that Nevadans liked him.

Nineteen fifty was my last year with the Nevada State Fish and Game Commission. Early in 1949, at the request of the state commission, the school board had granted me a final one-year leave-of-absence, and I had asked the commission to appoint an assistant director who would take my place in 1950. Frank Groves, who was highly qualified with a master's degree in wildlife management and several years of experience with the U.S. Fish and Wildlife Service, was hired, and I worked with Frank for the next year. I had remained with the fish and game commission longer than the Major had originally advised. He understood the reasons but was pleased when I returned to teaching in September of 1950.

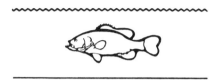

In May of 1947, the *New York Times* had reported, "The 168-foot steel yacht, *Haida,* built for Major Max C. Fleischmann of Glenbrook, Nev., and one of the largest pleasure crafts built since the war, was launched today at the Bath Iron Works Corporation." In the fall of that year, I had received a note (undated) from Mrs. Fleischmann which included, "The *Haida* started west the 31st and should be in Santa Barbara on the 16th or 17th. Many thrills when we see her." Another *New York Times* article on September 2 said, "Major Max C. Fleischmann today accepted delivery of the *Haida,* [a] 168-foot turbine yacht. The craft, which was brought through the Panama Canal from Bath, Maine, will have as its skipper Capt. D. N. Welch. . . . Major Fleischmann was so eager to see it that he flew his airplane out to sea and buzzed the crew as the yacht rounded Anacapa Island."

During the last two weeks of April 1951, Morley Griswold and his son Bill accompanied the Major on the *Haida* to fish Mexican waters. Morley, a former governor of Nevada, was a close friend of the Fleischmanns and an expert, all-around outdoorsman. In 1946, at the junction of the Deschutes and Columbia rivers in Oregon, he landed a twenty-eight-pound steelhead—at that time the world record steelhead caught on fly tackle. Bill was not far behind his father in his capability with a shotgun and a fly rod.

Bill told me of an incident on the trip which demonstrated the Major's dedication to conservation and sportsmanship. Fishing in the Gulf of California south of La Paz, they anchored in a bay near what is now known as Buena Vista, and were treated to an unusual and interesting sight. Feeding in the bay were a number of whale sharks, the world's largest fish. Bill estimated that the ones he saw were twenty to thirty feet in length. Although they are sharks, they are entirely harmless, feeding on plankton—tiny plant and animal life found in the oceans as well as in freshwater lakes and streams. Brown in color with small white spots, the whale sharks could be watched as they cruised along close to the surface, scooping in plankton.

During the afternoon another yacht, owned by a man the Major knew quite well, came into the bay and lowered several small fishing boats. A short time later the *Haida* party began hearing high-powered rifle shots and wondered what the targets could be.

That evening the Major and his party were invited over to the other yacht for cocktails. Shortly after their arrival, their host mentioned that the rifle fire had been directed at whale sharks. Bill said that the Major's face turned red, and that he did not mince any words on how he felt about that kind of vicious killing. Pointing out that the huge fish were rare creatures which provided pleasure to those fortunate enough to see them, he said that it was hard to believe that anyone would shoot them just to be killing something. He then called for his launch and the *Haida* party left the yacht.

The next morning he ordered Captain Welch to attempt to drive the whale sharks out of the bay into deeper and safer water and said that he would never again fish in the same area in which the other ship was fishing.

During the trip they had excellent marlin fishing, but the Major allowed them to keep only two of the fish to give to his native friends. The others were released unharmed.

Bill concluded, "I don't think the Major killed anything just for the sake of killing. He was a fine sportsman and a darned good conservationist. If a person was not a top-grade sportsman, he could not expect to retain the respect and friendship of the Major."

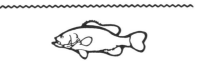

I was never able to hunt with the Major. In the fall when the upland bird and waterfowl seasons opened, I was working, and he had moved to his estate in South Carolina. Occasionally one of his friends would mention his ability with a shotgun, but it was not until I read Jimmy Robinson's article in *The American Shotgunner* that I learned of Max Fleischmann's national reputation.[1]

Few experienced trapshooters have not heard of the famous Jimmy Robinson or read his articles in *Sports Afield*. He is the author of fourteen books and the only outdoorsman in six halls of fame—the American Trapshooting, National Skeet Shooting, National Fishing, Minnesota Sports, Minnesota Skeet, and Minnesota State Trapshooting halls of fame. His shooting friends included Annie Oakley, Ernest Hemingway, Grantland Rice, Jack Dempsey, Barron Hilton, Gary Cooper, Clark Gable, Babe Ruth, Max Fleischmann, and many other famous people.

Robinson's article began: "Major Max Fleischmann—one of Ducks Unlimited's greatest friends—was a master at all he attempted. Fleischmann was a crack shot, both at clay pigeons and in the field. To this day, I consider him one of the greatest quail shots I ever joined in the field."

Jimmy and the Major first met in the mid 1920s at a shoot in Kentucky when Jimmy was statistician and assistant manager of the Amateur Trapshooting Association of Vandalia, Ohio. It was his job to keep track of the top shooters in the nation and report the results from both live-pigeon shoots and trapshooting to *Sports Afield* magazine. According to Jimmy Robinson, Fleischmann was twenty-one years old when he joined the Cincinnati Gun Club. He quickly developed into a fine shot and soon established himself as a truly great shooter.

This master was still a top shot 50 years later when I watched him score countless doubles on upland quail with his little Purdey .410 at his Hope Plantation in South Carolina. I've shot with some of the nation's greatest quail shooters in my time, and Max Fleischmann didn't take a back seat to any of them.

When Jimmy again met this "internationally famed sportsman," they were both vitally involved with developing Ducks Unlimited. He recalls his impression of Max: "A short, bushy eyebrowed, white-haired bundle of energy. His earlier years as a lightweight boxer, and later a semi-professional baseball player, showed in his every movement."

Major Fleischmann enjoyed bringing his friends to the Hope Plantation to shoot both ducks and quail, and Jimmy received an invitation at a Ducks Unlimited convention when the Major said, "Why don't you and Clara have a hunt with me this fall? Shoot yourself a mess of quail before you get too old, Jimmy!" Jimmy and his wife Clara went to the plantation after he closed his own duck hunting club in the winter of 1950. He wrote:

> The plantation was located about 40 miles outside of Charleston and embraced some 8,000 acres on the side of a huge cypress swamp. The mansion itself was splendid, with oak trees gracing the buildings, each laden with Spanish moss. Nearby were the Major's cornfields and his kennels that were the home to 50 or more hunting dogs. It was only half a mile to his duck slough that was always loaded with greenheads. The plantation mansion was staffed by servants, all of whom loved the Major and his charming wife, Sarah. They kept appearing at odd moments to answer your every wish for food and drink. It was pleasant then and pleasant in my memory. I can still see this snow-thatched master of the estate literally bounding up the winding staircase to fetch photographs of one of his better hunts, so we could enjoy it with him.

Nor will I forget the Currier and Ives original art that adorned the walls. We would sit and talk about his hunting dogs, some of the finest I've yet hunted over and, of course, we would discuss our mutual love of Ducks Unlimited and the great work this fine organization was doing in conservation. He was DU's greatest contributor at that time.

Jimmy and the Major, with their mutual sports interests and their enjoyment of cigars, became instant friends. Cuban cigars were always in a cedar box on his dining room table, and next to it was a box of ten-cent cigars. Jimmy said that Max would patiently explain,

"We smoke the Cuban cigars after dinner, but you can fill your pockets with the ten-centers for the hunt." Somehow on the first hunt morning, I made a slight mistake. I got my fingers into Max's dollar cigars before we started the day. Every time Max would down a double with his trusty .410, he would turn to me and chuckle—and I, with a dollar cigar stuck in my mouth, would smile back. After the shoot was over the head dog handler whispered to me, "The Major out shot you, Jimmy, but you sure as hell out smoked him."

Max was a great all-round sportsman. When his good friend, Teddy Roosevelt, wanted to make an African expedition, it was Max who mapped out the trip.

The Major owned an array of expensive American and foreign rifles and shotguns, and one time when one of his favorite English Purdey shotguns broke down and his New York gunsmith was unable to fix it, he flew directly to London to see the maker and have his gun repaired. He had to wait there three weeks, and Jimmy asked him what he did to pass the time. "I shot at the London Gun Club nearly every day and went to night clubs every night," he replied.

Another of Jimmy's stories tells of the day the Major was about to leave on a hunting trip. Certain Fleischmann interests were about to be sold—a deal involving millions of dollars. The lawyers delayed somehow, finally locating the Major just as he was about to get aboard a train. He told them to hold off the deal until he returned.

Jimmy said that the Major first became interested in Ducks Unlimited when he was invited to western Canada to inspect some of the young organization's projects. Noting that they were using horses and drag lines to move the earth, he suggested a huge Cat tractor—which he soon donated. It was used for many years and was fondly named "The Major" by D.U. men.

In Jimmy Robinson's book, *The Best Of Jimmy Robinson*, there is a photograph of Major Max Fleischmann. The last sentence of its caption reads, "Of all the sportsmen I have ever known the Major ranked among the top."[2]

Jimmy was the last sportsman to hunt with the Major. I was the last to fish with him.

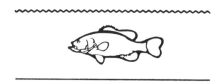

It was in August of 1951 that Nevada and I had our "once-in-a-lifetime" trip. The Major and Mrs. Fleischmann moved from Santa Barbara to the Jacks Valley Ranch in late June, and they called to ask that I come out to see them as soon as it was convenient. I had to drive to Carson City several days later, and so continued on to Jacks Valley. While we visited in their living room, I sensed that they had something to tell me. Finally the Major said, "Mrs. Fleischmann and I wish you and Nevada to go to Alaska on the *Haida* with us in August."

I was surprised and very pleased, and when I reached home and told Nevada, she asked so many questions that she burned the dinner.

I did have a problem concerning the beginning of the school year, but a local travel agency found that we could get passage on a tourist ship at Ketchikan on August 25 or 27, which would get us back in time. I wrote the Major about it, assuring him that if the plan would cause inconvenience, I would arrange for a substitute teacher.

On July 9 he replied:

> Just had your letter of July 7th. The plan you outline, viz, catching a boat in Ketchikan on either August 25th or 27th, will be entirely agreeable to me and will fit in with my plans, so don't worry in any way about putting us out.
>
> I am sleeping on the plane at the Reno Airport the night of July 11th as I have to be at a bank meeting that morning and am leaving about 4:30 or 4:45 the morning of the twelfth for a week's fishing in New Mexico. I don't look forward to it with too much zest as far as the fishing is concerned, as when I was originally invited there were only three or four men. Now the party has grown to fifteen.
>
> I have been fortunate in getting one of the McKenzie fishing guides who has been with me on a number of fishing trips up north and who was awfully good in helping across bad pieces of water, tieing flies, etc. He is going to join the *Haida* at Seattle on August 1st.

At ten o'clock on the morning of August 2, the *Silver Falcon*, with Captain Ash and Dan Withers at the controls, was rolling down the Reno airport runway; in seconds we were climbing into blue, clear skies. Nevada had never flown before, and she held my hand very tight; but by the time Oregon's majestic peaks came into sight, she was relaxed and enjoying the scenery. At twelve-thirty we were touching down at the Seattle airport where Captain Dave Welch was waiting for us. Less than an hour later we had our first sight of the *Haida*.

I had not seen a photograph of the ship, and, as it lay alongside its dock in Lake Washington, my first thought was

109

that it resembled a miniature ocean liner. The seventeen officers and crew were lined up near the gangplank waiting to greet the Major, and he spoke to each of them as he passed by.

Nevada and I were shown to our quarters which, except for one other stateroom, were the only guest accommodations on the ship. Later, Captain Welch explained that it had been built that way because the Major disliked traveling for any long period of time with more than one fishing companion.

When we were settled in our pleasant and comfortable double stateroom, Mrs. Fleischmann gave us a short tour of the yacht. I knew so little about ships that I later referred to a pamphlet written by John H. Wells, the designer of the *Haida.* He wrote:

> Long envisaged by Major Max C. Fleischmann, who during his lifetime built twenty-two yachts . . . Bath Iron Works set about building her, sparing neither talent, detail or expense, to make her the fastest and finest seagoing vessel of her size and type. The *Haida* is a vessel of unusual cruise capacity—permitting her to sail to Europe and return to the United States on only one filling of tanks. She is designed for sea worthiness as well as comfort, and is outstanding in both.[3]

The dining room was finished in a beautiful wood I did not recognize, and I asked Mrs. Fleischmann, who said it was bleached primavera. The salon, twenty-seven by fourteen feet, was equipped with an electric-heat fireplace, roomy bookcases, and finished in natural teak throughout. It opened to a thirty-foot covered afterdeck, furnished with a full-length stern seat, deck chairs, tables, and similar items conducive to relaxation. Below deck the owner's quarters consisted of three double staterooms, two of which (the Major's and Mrs. Fleischmann's) were the full width of the ship and complete with baths, dressing rooms, etc.

Outside, there were four small boats: two power launches (one a fast twenty-six-foot owner's fishing launch) and two fourteen-foot dinghies. The *Haida* was equipped with every modern accessory in use at that time. Radar, the Sperry gyro-automatic steering device and course recorder, the fathometer, RCA long- and short-wave radio, wireless telephone, direction finder, and searchlights were included in the ship's modern communications equipment.

It was a beautiful ship both inside and outside.

That evening Frank Dufresne, whom I knew (he was associate editor of *Field and Stream* magazine which in 1947 had published one of my stories), and Mrs. Dufresne came aboard for dinner. The Major showed Frank the tackle room, which had the appearance of a small sporting goods store.

Fortunately Nevada had a small notebook in which she jotted down dates and places and other general events of the trip. According to her "diary," the *Haida* left her Seattle berth at eight o'clock the next morning. I remember awakening to the soft hum of the powerful diesel motors. We went on deck as the *Haida* passed through the Chittenden locks; a large number of people were watching the beautiful ship from shore. Captain Welch, handsome in his spotless uniform, was on the bow making certain the ship did not scrape the sides of the locks, and I heard Mrs. Fleischmann whisper to Nevada, "He probably has a good-looking girl friend in that crowd." A moment later, as he leaned over the side, a fresh breeze caught the rim of his hat, and it dropped over the side. A groan of sympathy came from the crowd, but the captain kept his composure.

That evening we anchored in Departure Bay, and were headed north again early the next morning, anchoring at Port Hardy on the northern tip of Vancouver Island; the Major, guide Jack Lowry, and I went ashore in one of the small boats to obtain our British Columbia fishing licenses.

During the following morning we crossed Queen Charlotte Strait to enter Rivers Inlet where we anchored near two other yachts, one of which belonged to a friend of the Fleischmanns, Bill Boeing of the aircraft company. Hanging above the afterdeck of the second yacht was a king (chinook) salmon which must have weighed between sixty and seventy pounds.

That evening Mr. and Mrs. Boeing and their guests, Mr. and Mrs. Joseph Ripley, came on board the *Haida* for cocktails. Before returning to their ship, *The Black Prince*, the Boeings invited us over for dinner the following evening.

After breakfast the next morning, I found that the two small boats with outboard motors had been lowered into the water beside the *Haida*. Jack Lowry would guide the Major, and the first mate, Pete, would handle the motor for me.

Rivers Inlet was famous for its large salmon; record fish had been caught there year after year. Because I had landed twenty-pound salmon on light tackle on the Klamath and Rogue Rivers in California and Oregon, I made the unwise decision to use a five-ounce rod.

We had been trolling about twenty minutes when I had the first strike. In seconds the fish was free. When the same thing happened on the next two strikes, I knew what was wrong—my rod was too light to set the hook in the tough, large jaws of those big fish, and I decided that when we returned to the *Haida* for lunch, I would take a heavier rod for the afternoon fishing.

About ten o'clock, two boats came out from the yacht on which we had seen the big salmon hanging. Shortly, one of their occupants yelled loudly, "Fish on! Fish on!" Men in the other boat started calling advice in loud voices; finally the fish broke loose. From then on, the bay echoed with their calls and comments to each other, and I began to worry—guessing what the Major was thinking. He was tolerant of many things, but amateurish fishing behavior was not one of them.

We returned to the *Haida* and were starting lunch when I heard the sound of the anchor being raised. Mrs. Fleischmann asked, "Are we moving the *Haida*, dear?"

The Major answered, "We're leaving here. There's some damn amateurs out there yelling like a bunch of school kids."

Mrs. Fleischmann, showing her surprise, said, "But we've been invited to the Boeings for dinner."

The Major ended the discussion with, "I've sent Franzen [John Franzen, the steward] over to tell them we are headed up the coast."

That evening we were anchored in another inlet which, according to Nevada's spelling, was known as Kakusdish. Before dinner the Major and I were fighting coho (silver) salmon which, with their aerial acrobatics, were more sport than the larger chinooks.

The next day one of the crew took Nevada fishing, furnishing her with one of the Major's salt-water rods. She hooked and landed a nice coho, but when she returned to the *Haida* the Major said, "I don't know who fitted you out with that rod, but it's like hunting rabbits with an elephant gun. The next time you fish, you let me choose the rod."

Coho were jumping, so I tried a fly rod with steelhead flies. I lost leaders and flies, but it was great sport.

The fish we caught went into the ship's walk-in freezer to be stored until the end of the trip when they would be divided among the officers and crew for their winter fish dinners.

That afternoon (August 8) we continued on northward to another of the Major's favorite places, Lowes Inlet. Nevada wrote in her notebook, "The scenery is beautiful. High wooded mountains, stretching right down to the bay, seem so close you could almost touch them."

The following morning, the Major had a different type of fishing planned. A river entered the inlet over a waterfall, and before we had finished breakfast, the crew had carried a fourteen-foot boat and an outboard motor over a path around the waterfall to a lake above it. We were to fly-fish for cutthroat trout in a stream entering the upper end of the lake. As I remember, the lake was about two miles long.

While I was getting my fly tackle together, the Major handed me a small, wooden landing net. I thanked him but said that if we were stream fishing I would not need it. He insisted it would be of use, so rather than further discuss it, I included it in my gear.

The lake was smooth, and with Jack handling the motor, we landed in about an hour on a rocky shore near the mouth of a good-sized stream. Jack, not fishing, stayed with the Major, and I let them go ahead while I tried a small riffle not far from the lake. I had a dropper fly as well as an end fly on my leader, and two fourteen-inch cutthroats each grabbed a fly and decided to go in opposite directions. The leader parted, and from then on I fished with one fly.

I found the Major, with Jack beside him, fishing a riffle from a rocky reef which extended across the stream. The Major signaled me to try the far side of the reef, and I waded across and hooked a fish on the first cast. After tiring it out, I brought the trout into shallow water and removed the hook from its jaw.

The Major asked, "Where is your net?"

I looked for it; I did not have it. I said, "I must have left it downstream."

Well, I don't remember exactly what the Major said, but it had something to do with the need for people to be extra careful with borrowed equipment.

Probably because he had never said anything like that during the many years we had fished together, I was surprised and annoyed. I said, "Major, you know damn well that I did not want that net, but you insisted. In the first place, as you should know, I never use a net unless I'm in a boat because I can release a fish without the damage it receives flopping around in a net. And second, I don't like to borrow fishing tackle or anything else."

The Major said something about borrowing being sometimes necessary, but he let the matter drop, and I went on fishing. A few minutes later I tied into a fish that was too big to be in that stream, and when it started down with the current, it easily took my leader with it. For the rest of the day the Major was especially pleasant. The net was never again mentioned.

On arriving back at the *Haida* in late afternoon, we learned that the first mate had caught three coho below the waterfall. So the Major, with Jack operating the boat, gave it a half-hour try and brought back a good-sized fish.

The next morning (August 10) the *Haida* headed for Ketchikan. During the days that we traveled, I developed a routine which was enjoyable. After an eight o'clock breakfast with at least twelve different choices on the menu, I would spend an hour or two in the pilot house watching Captain Dave Welch and Pete, the first mate, handle the *Haida*. The captain told some interesting stories of his war years when he commanded convoys of ships crossing the ocean. He was an interesting person, and I got to know him quite well.

About ten o'clock I would be invited down to the crew's mess for coffee and the most delicious rolls I have ever eaten. The *Haida*'s baker was well known as an expert in his profession, and regardless of the more than ample breakfast I had consumed, I looked forward to ten o'clock. Maybe it was the salt air.

Usually the remainder of the morning was spent on deck enjoying the beauty of the Inland Passage. Occasionally there would be a totem pole visible among the trees above the shore, and one morning I saw a killer whale, the largest member of the dolphin family, leap clear of the water with its white underside and long dorsal fin glistening in the sunlight.

Both luncheon and dinner were served formally, with beautiful china and sparkling silver; but when we had been fishing, the Major and I often sat down at the table in still-damp waders. Dinner aboard the *Haida*, in both food and service, excelled any restaurant dining I had ever experienced.

Mrs. Fleischmann and Nevada enjoyed playing cards, and during some afternoons when the *Haida* was moving northward, I would join them for an hour or so. During the evenings, I often used the Major's library.

The radio was never turned on during news broadcasts. Mrs. Fleischmann said that on trips into natural environments, the Major wished to leave behind the tragedies and politics of the rest of the world.

Through the years that I had known Major and Mrs. Fleischmann, I really knew very little about their personal lives. I had admired Mrs. Fleischmann's interest in our Nevada fishing trips—invariably she met us at the yard gate to learn whether we had been successful; and I was pleased when the Major described to her our experiences of the day. But it was during the month-long Alaskan trip that I learned the depth of their friendship, something they may have gained during the hardships they had faced together on their expeditions to the primitive areas of the earth. Mrs. Fleischmann was a diabetic; the Major's concern for her condition and her regard for his comfort were always apparent. Regardless of anything else, there was a deep gentleness and kindness which they had retained through almost a half-century of marriage.

While it was not exactly sport fishing, the *Haida*'s first mate and sometimes members of the crew would drop a heavy line with a large baited hook over the side of the ship whenever it anchored in an attempt to catch a halibut. One day when we were returning from fishing we saw a commotion on the deck with several of the crew helping the mate lift a huge flatfish up the side of the *Haida*. I do not remember how much it weighed, but when it went into the freezer it added many halibut steaks to the crew's store of winter dinners.

Nevada's small notebook outlines our trip from August 10 through 15.

Aug. 10 (Sunny)
    Arrived in Ketchikan today about 3:30. Buck, Jack and I went up town, a funny little city, and bought some gifts. A doctor came on board to see the Major who hasn't been feeling well. Very warm in Ketchikan.

Aug. 11

Left Ketchikan about noon for Hump Back Bay and Anan river [where the Major wanted us to see bears catching salmon]. Anchored about five o'clock. Jack, Buck and I went ashore in outboard boat and hiked up Anan River. Humpback salmon were migrating up the river to spawn, literally millions—stream was black with them—have never seen such a sight. Hoped to see some bear but were disappointed. It is the most beautiful trail I have ever seen—looks like a fairyland with lichen covered trees, fern and moss undergrowth. Came back at 7 for dinner. [The Major sent us] back up at eight and we saw 12 bears in river fishing for humpback salmon. We sat on rock and watched them—two were very close. One was old brown colored bear—would grab salmon with teeth. Amazing sight. When we were about to leave, Buck said hello to closest one, and they all started running across the river. Back at *Haida* mate had caught a halibut—queer looking fish. Today was a beautiful day. But Major feeling poorly.

Sunday Aug. 12

First cloudy day. Left Hump Back and Anan at 8 o'clock—arrived at Thorne Bay about 11 o'clock. Had to wind around beautiful mountain to get into Thorne Bay which is smooth as glass and reflects the mountains all around.

Buck and Jack went up mountain stream to fish about 11:30—got back about 6 P.M.. Kept 30 of the lovely cutthroat and then released 89. Crew went out with a crab net this P.M. about 4 and came in with 30 lovely crabs. Sun doesn't go down until 9:34.

Monday Aug. 13

Came back to Ketchikan as the Major was feeling very bad. Doctor came aboard at 9:30—took Major to hospital for x-rays and observation. Mrs. Fleischmann, Buck and I went in at 2. He is better—x-rays show stomach congestion. Took ride around Ketchikan—

back to hospital—back to *Haida*. Today we have had much rain—first day.

Tuesday Aug. 14 Ketchikan.
Nice day. Went to hospital. Major about the same. Went with Captain Welch shopping for pillow for Major—got an all-down. Mrs. Fleischmann went back to see doctor. Major about the same.

Wed. Aug. 15 Ketchikan
Went in at 11 to meet Mrs. Fleischmann at hospital. She says the Major said he is a little better. Have hair appointment this evening. We are all concerned about Mrs. Fleischmann—they are such wonderful people. Major came back on board at 3:30. We left Ketchikan at 4:15 headed north. Anchored in Slenmer Bay at almost 9:30 P.M.

Thurs. Aug. 16
Left call for 7:30 to see Wrangell Narrows. Very difficult to get through—has to be at low tide. Passed Wrangell and Petersberg. Saw Patterann glacier and Bear glacier—also saw some icebergs and 2 seals. Arrived Pavlof about 5:30. Buck and Jack went out salmon fishing. Pete, the mate, caught a 75 lb. halibut off side of boat. Left Pavlof and arrive Basket Bay on Chichagof Island.

The Major wanted Nevada and me to see a cave along the cliff-like shoreline. In a small boat, Jack took us into the cave where the water was so clear that we could see fish swimming over the white, sandy bottom. It was like a large aquarium, and Nevada thought it was a beautiful sight.

Later, the Major arranged for Jack and me to follow a trail up a stream which flowed into Basket Bay. He told us that we would find that the stream emerged from a natural tunnel where both cutthroat and spawning sockeye would be found. Apparently he had decided that he was not well enough to go, but he had told me about this place and wished me to see it.

It was raining, so we wore slickers, and the Major had Jack carry a large-caliber rifle because of the possibility of encountering one of Chichagof's Alaskan brown bears, which usually were dangerous only if surprised, cornered, or wounded.

The bay was rough, and the trip in the fourteen-foot outboard in a heavy rain was a little tricky for the crew member who took us to shore. In less than an hour's hike, we came to the tunnel the Major had described. It was difficult to cast into the tunnel, but we managed to catch a few small trout before I hooked a heavy fish. When I finally worked it into the daylight I saw that it was a beautiful male sockeye salmon, its sides a brilliant red. My fly had hooked its pectoral fin, and it put up a strong fight before I was able to get it into shallow water and release it.

When we returned to the shore, we signaled the *Haida* for the small boat, and shortly after 5:00 P.M. we were on our way to Whitewater Bay on Admiralty Island to fish for Dolly Varden trout. That evening I had a slight pain in my right side.

I'll never forget the briefing Jack and I received the next morning. We were in our waders in the salon where the Major was sitting in his favorite chair. After warning us about the Alaskan brown bears which bedded down in the tall grass of an area we had to cross, he gave us the following instructions—I believe I almost remember his exact words.

> You will find a long length of rope in your boat, and when you reach shore you are to fasten it to the prow and then pull it to its full length up the shore, where you will tie it to a tree. When you return to the boat you will understand why you have done this.
>
> As you hike up the river you will come to a large hole which looks as if it should be full of fish, but you will not have a single strike there. Knowing what damn-fool fishermen you both are, you will probably try it, but you will just waste your time.

Eventually you will come to a second hole, and, regardless of what I say, you will try again.

You will then go through the high grass (it is taller than you are), and that is where you should be careful not to surprise a brown bear. When you come to the stream again you will look for a log which has fallen across it—that tree trunk has been there for all the years I've fished the stream—and from that point on you will catch Dolly Vardens.

We thanked him and headed for our boat, which the crew had lowered. When we reached the shore, we followed the Major's suggestion and dragged the full length of rope (it must have been several hundred feet long) up the bank and tied it to a tree.

I think Jack and I were about the same age, and when we fished together there ceased to be a guide and guest; we were just two "damn-fool fishermen." We came to the first hole, and I looked at Jack. He nodded his head, and we started casting flies. We didn't have a single rise. At the second hole, it was the same routine.

We reached the area of the high grass and about halfway across came to a small clearing where the grass was flattened to the ground; steam was still rising from where a huge animal had been lying. The enormous footprints un-doubtedly were those of an Alaskan brown bear. Jack and I had made a point of talking loudly—the bear had heard us coming.

We came to the Major's log, and, sure enough, Jack was soon tied into a three- to four-pound, beautifully colored Dolly Varden—very similar in appearance to an Eastern brook trout. Before Jack landed his, I had one on, and for the next hour we had great sport. When we had caught seven apiece, we headed for the boat. Pain in my right side made me walk bent over.

On reaching the shore we saw our boat floating several hundred feet (it looked like half a mile) out in the bay. The tide had come in and the water was not far below the tree to which we had tied the rope.

When we got back to the *Haida*, we learned that some of the crew had gone ashore and returned with two sacks full of clams. There was no lack of sea food in coastal Alaska.

Mrs. Fleischmann had two Siamese cats which she had named "Brother" and "Sister." Both of them were very curious and managed to get into considerable trouble. Although Nevada had hung her knitting bag high above the floor, one day she saw Brother's head sticking out of it with a tangled mass of yarn wrapped around his neck. Nevada's notebook reads,

> During afternoon Brother got through netting strung around afterdeck to keep cats from falling overboard. He was hanging on to net—over water—with one paw. There was great excitement with crew starting to lower boat, when I reached through net and pulled him in. Saw a whale tonight and watched most beautiful sunset I've ever seen. Buck really feeling poorly.

The next morning, I was really sick. The captain felt my right side and said he thought it was my appendix. The Major told him to head for Wrangell where there was a doctor and a hospital. Because it was Sunday, the captain called ahead by wireless telephone, and a Doctor Beisel and a nurse were waiting for me when I reached the hospital.

After a thorough examination, including blood and other tests, the doctor confirmed the captain's diagnosis and recommended immediate surgery. I explained that surgery would end the only trip of its kind I could ever hope to have, and asked if there was any alternative.

He was a young doctor, and I could see that he understood. He was silent for a few minutes and finally said, "I'll give you a heavy dose of penicillin and a bottle of sulpha tablets. If your pain gets worse, your ship can call me, and I'll fly out and remove your appendix aboard the *Haida*. The salt air and a clean ship make a fairly sterile surgery."

Well, I was delighted. When I took out my wallet to pay for at least two hours of his and the nurse's time, plus two shots of penicillin and a large bottle of sulpha tablets, I hoped that I had enough cash with me.

The doctor did his arithmetic on a small piece of paper, and mentioning the nurse's compensation, said, "I'm afraid I'll have to charge you eight dollars." It was the only time I ever asked a doctor to increase his fee, but he would not change the amount.

When I had left the *Haida* it had floated near the top of the pier, but when I returned, it was so far below it that I had to climb down a long ladder—an example of the exceptional tides in that part of Alaska.

That evening the steward, John Franzen, secretly gave me a handful of antibiotic capsules he had in his kit. They probably did not help, but I took them along with the sulpha.

I still have my appendix.

I was feeling a little better the next morning (August 20), but the Major had become worse during the night, and we again headed for Ketchikan—arriving in midafternoon in time for the Major's doctor to again examine him. This time the doctor strongly recommended that the *Haida* turn south.

Nevada and I cancelled our reservations for returning home on a tour ship, and the next morning we were headed for the United States. Any desire for more fishing had evaporated; all of us wished only to get the Major back to the best specialists. But we soon found out that he would not cooperate. When we reached Lowes Inlet that afternoon, he told the captain that we would anchor there for a day or so.

A treaty, going back many years, gave a tribe of Indians the exclusive right to commercially fish a narrow, short stretch of the inlet from below the main waterfall to where it widened into a bay. The Indians had stretched a rope across the boundary, and only sportsmen in small boats were allowed to fish beyond it. During the evening we watched Indians using their nets below the waterfall.

The next morning we saw that the Indians had left the inlet, and the Major requested that Jack and I give it a try. We knew we could not refuse; we hoped that the Indians had thinned out the fish, and that we would not get a strike. It was not fly-fishing water, so I used a light spinning rod with a spoon lure. Jack worked the boat up within casting distance of the base of the waterfall, and within the next hour we caught two coho. The second one, a sixteen-pounder, was a strong fish, and I landed it about fifty yards from the *Haida;* the Major, with field glasses, was watching us from the afterdeck, which made us feel sad that he was unable to fish with us.

After lunch the Major asked me to do some exploring for him. Stewart Edward White, the famous author whose books included his adventures in the Arctic, Africa, and the West, had been a friend of the Major and had shared his enthusiasm for British Columbian and Alaskan coastal waters. Before Mr. White's death in 1946, he had given the Major his maps of the coastal areas he had fished, and one of them showed a stream entering the Inland Passage not far from Lowes Inlet.

The first mate would take Jack and me in the *Haida Papoose* (the twenty-six-foot fast launch) to a small bay where there was no landing area. They would have to drop us offshore into water which we hoped would not be deeper than our waders. The map gave explicit directions and stated that White had marked a trail, which followed the stream up a canyon, with blazes on tree trunks.

By the time Jack and I had donned our wading gear, we found that the *Papoose* had been lowered, with Pete and a sailor waiting for us. We carried a pair of hiking shoes but no fishing tackle. It was a beautiful launch with a powerful motor (the captain called it "the Major's hot rod"), and we were soon skimming out of the inlet and down the Inland Passage. Pete had been thoroughly briefed by the Major, and it was not long before we were creeping slowly into a small bay. Jack and I climbed onto the decking over the prow and hung from the side as the mate inched the boat towards the shore. The water was so clear that I could see that the bottom of the bay was covered with clams, packed so tightly together that the sand and rocks were barely visible. Suddenly the mate called, "O.K., drop now."

I don't know how he judged the depth so accurately. When my feet touched and crushed clam shells, the water reached to within two inches of the top of my waders. Saying he would pick us up in about two hours, Pete headed the *Papoose* back towards the *Haida.* Jack and I waded to shore where we changed our waders for hiking shoes.

About a hundred yards up the stream, we found the first blaze on a trunk of a tree where White had chopped off a rectangular slab of bark to reveal the lighter wood. The trail was faint, apparently used only by animals, but we found blazes about one hundred yards apart.

The canyon rose sharply towards what appeared to be a pass in the mountains, and we kept a fast pace to get as far as possible before we would have to turn back to meet the launch. It had been a very dry year, and we found no area of the stream with enough water to allow a spawning migration of salmon or cutthroat trout—in places the streambed was almost dry. Finally, we had to turn back. When we reached the bay, the *Papoose* was waiting for us.

The Major was quite interested in our report and seemed satisfied with it. I noticed that he seemed weak and unsteady on his feet. We had learned that he disliked people asking how he felt, but we had a way of determining his condition. After dinner, the steward would bring him a Havana cigar. If he was in pain, he would say, "A good cigar would be wasted. Bring me a ten-center."

It was that evening that, against Mrs. Fleischmann's and the captain's advice, the Major decided to fish below the waterfall. The captain sent word that he wished to see me in the pilot house, and when I arrived, Jack and the first mate were there. They were all worried, especially about the Major falling out of the small boat when he stood up to cast. Dave Welch said that it was his responsibility, and, as captain of the ship, he would tell the Major that he would not allow it.

Several days earlier, Dave had told me that on a Mexican trip, the Major had lost his temper and fired him when he refused to increase the ship's speed in heavy seas. A half-hour later the Major had apologized and rehired him.

I said, "Dave it will not do any good. He will probably fire you and then rehire you when he gets back from fishing. Let me talk to him; I have nothing to lose."

I found the Major resting on the couch in his office. I sat down and said, "Major, I've noticed you are very unsteady on your feet. You definitely should not fish from that small boat." He started to reply, but I continued, "Major, you will have Mrs. Fleischmann, the officers and crew, and all the rest of us worried if you try it."

There was no indication of anger as he turned to me, and I believe I can almost quote his exact words. He said, "Buck, why in the world are they worried about me? I've had a damn good life. I've been every place I've wanted to go and done everything I've wanted to do. Most of these things I can't do anymore. I won't fall out of that boat, but if I did, I'd rather die here than in a hospital. And when I die no one should feel badly about it."

Well, maybe someone else could have given him a sensible answer, but I could not.

On the way back to the bridge, I thought of one safeguard if he did fall overboard, and, after telling the captain that I had failed to change his mind, I suggested that we attach a small but strong rope to one of the flotation cushions and tie the other end to the back of Jack's belt. Jack would sit on the rope, thus covering it from sight. We knew the Major would not wear a life preserver, but if he should fall overboard, Jack (who was a capable swimmer) could jump after him, dragging the flotation cushion with him. A second boat would be in the water, ready to immediately head for them. Everyone thought it was the best possibility, and we started putting the rigging together.

We watched from the *Haida* as Jack held the boat within casting distance of the waterfall. The Major would stand up to cast, and we could see him weave. But he caught a coho and came back quite pleased and satisfied. From then on everyone aboard the *Haida* had a single wish—get the Major back to the United States nonstop. But it was not to be.

Two hours out of Lowes Inlet, the Major sent word to the captain to drop anchor off of what he called Seven Mile Creek. He told Jack and me to get into our waders and hike a mile or so up the creek to see if any salmon were in. The anchor hit the bottom about the same time our boat touched the water, and a few minutes later we were on shore and on our way. When we were out of sight of the Major, we increased our walking to almost a jog. The stream was low; we saw no indication of fish, and we headed back. When we described the condition of the stream, he believed us, and we were on our way again—but not for long.

At Indian Creek he stopped the *Haida,* and Jack and I went ashore to where a natural dam made a waterfall into a large pool below it. Because of the current drought, the barrier was insurmountable, and the pool below it was so choked with humpbacks that it was impossible to fish.

Starting back for the shore we saw a large commercial fishing ship anchored off of the mouth of the stream. Canadian markers declaring the stream off-limits to commercial fishing were in clear view. As we were passing a large boulder, I noticed netting protruding from a hollow beneath it. We pulled on it until a very large seine with weights attached slid out into the open—it was still wet. Undoubtedly the fishing ship was waiting for us to leave before illegally seining the hundreds of salmon congregated in the pool.

Jack was conservation oriented, and it had been less than a year since I had been helping to enforce the game laws of Nevada. The adrenalin which started flowing in both of us encouraged a course of action which was not the wisest we could have chosen.

There were a half-dozen or so men, some with field glasses, watching us from the large ship as we dragged the seine down to the edge of the water. Pulling about half of it into the boat, with the remainder dragging behind, we headed into the center of the Inland Passage where the water was black from its depth. We pushed the netting in the boat overboard, and its heavy weights quickly pulled it towards the bottom; it soon disappeared.

We were not far from the *Haida*, and when we went aboard we saw the Major, his field glasses hanging from his neck, waiting for us. There was a hint of amusement in his eyes, but he said, "Did you two wild-eyed conservationists stop for a moment to think that you should have left that seine where it was and called Canadian officials? They would have had a plane here in a short enough time to catch those S.O.B.s in the act." We both knew he was right.

According to Nevada's diary, we continued on to

Nowish Cove, a lovely harbor. Watched Pete the mate catch a fifteen pound halibut.

Aug. 24 Friday (sunny)
   We left Nowish at 7:30 P.M., arrived at Kakusdish at 10:30. Major a bit better. Went out with Jack—reported only humpies jumping—no coho. Left at 12 for McLaughlin Bay. Went by former Indian village of Bella Bella—now a little town.

Aug. 25 Sat. (foggy)
   Left at 8:30—anchored at Koeye. Major had Buck and Jack go ashore to Indian hut to find out if there were any fish in bay. Major is not improving. Seems quite weak. When Jack and Buck were coming back a humpie jumped in their boat. They threw it back into water— humpies are really jumping out here—no coho.

Left Koeye—through Queen Charlotte Straight it was rough. The *Haida* really rocked. Arrived Port Hardy around 5 P.M.

After dinner we noticed that the bay at Port Hardy was becoming dotted with small boats, and the Major asked us to go out to see if they were catching salmon. He said that he thought they probably were fishing for what they called "trout," which actually were small coho dropping down from spawning streams into the ocean.

In the small boat, we headed for the nearest fisherman and learned that the Major was correct. The angler said the boats were trolling small spinners; it was too early for coho—none had been seen.

I had two small spinners in my tackle box, and Jack and I put them on with the hope of catching and learning for certain the species of the small fish. We trolled for about fifteen minutes without a strike, and then headed toward the *Haida* to tell the Major there were no coho—which would be good news to everyone aboard.

Suddenly my rod tip almost hit Jack on the head, and a ten-pound coho—the first of the year—cleared the water in back of our boat. We could hardly believe it and hoped the Major was not watching so that we could release it and tell a white lie. I finally got the fish alongside the boat, and we saw the blood. The small lure had gone through and torn the gills and then hooked into the coho's eye. If we released it, it was certain to slowly die; we had to kill it and take it back. We were sick about it.

As we carried it aboard the *Haida*, the Major was waiting. When we explained that it was the first and only coho caught this season, we were relieved when he said that he guessed there was no use staying another day.

I remember later that evening, as I watched him sitting in his chair, that he seemed to be lost in thought. Then he turned to me and said very sincerely, "I'm glad, Buck, that you caught that coho." I have thought about that—the way he said it—many times in past years. We had caught so many salmon, I've wondered why he was so pleased about that last one. I hope it was not because he felt that it helped to compensate for some of the fishing he had planned for me which had been cut short by his illness. The fishing had been all anyone could wish for. I had seen beautiful rivers and mountains and back country, and it had been the trip of a lifetime for both Nevada and me.

Between Port Hardy and Departure Bay, a pod of killer whales (orcas) swam in a straight line parallel to the *Haida* for several miles. There were sixteen whales in the group, according to Nevada's diary. We passed through heavy smoke from forest fires burning on both Vancouver Island and on the mainland before we anchored in Departure Bay.

The next day we headed for Seattle. Because we would not arrive in time to fly to Reno that evening, the Major had the captain take a longer route which passed through some beautiful country.

We were on the afterdeck when the steward rushed out to tell us that the Major had fallen and was lying on the floor of his office. We found him there; he seemed to be unconscious, as if he had fainted. The *Haida* was passing through a fairly narrow stretch of the waterway, but the captain made a complete turn to head back to the shorter route to Seattle. He then came down to examine the Major, and finding no sign of broken bones, we moved him onto the couch. I stayed with him until we docked. He had regained consciousness; we would all stay aboard until morning.

I remember very clearly the departure from the *Haida*. The Major was dressed in slacks with a tie and sport coat. Mrs. Fleischmann took me aside to explain that the Major would go first, and she asked that I follow closely in back of him so that I could reach and steady him if he should stumble or slip. But my help was not needed. The old outdoorsman walked with his back as straight as if he were on a military parade ground. On deck he smiled and nodded to each member of the crew and shook hands with the captain. He did not falter as he walked across the gangplank. I felt proud of him.

We left Seattle in the *Silver Falcon* about ten o'clock the next morning, climbing through rain and towering cumulus clouds. The storm stretched as far as Reno, where we landed about one o'clock in a sixty-mile-an-hour wind. When the plane stopped in the unloading area, Captain Ash came back to learn how the Major was feeling. The Major greeted him with, "That was a damn rough trip, Captain."

Captain Ash had called ahead, and an ambulance was waiting to take the Major to Saint Mary's Hospital. I was standing near the *Silver Falcon* as the Major was being wheeled on a gurney toward the ambulance. I said, "Take care of yourself, Major."

He smiled and said, "I will, Buck."

It was the last time that I saw my fishing companion.

The Major was in Saint Mary's Hospital for several days. Dr. Fred Anderson and Dr. Fred Elliot were the physicians attending him before the *Silver Falcon* flew him to Santa Barbara's Cottage Hospital.

On September 15, we received a telegram from Mrs. Fleischmann: "All tests still negative. Have decided to perform exploratory operation early Monday afternoon. Will keep you informed. Love. Sarah Fleischmann."

On September 17, Julius Bergen wired: "Very bad news. Condition malignant in pancreas which could not be removed. [Mrs. Fleischmann] is bearing up well." Bergen wrote further on September 22:

> You and Nevada will want to know more about the details, and it is not a pretty picture. The surgeon found that the Major's entire pancreas is involved with a cancer, and it is hopeless to try to remove the tumor; it is very large. Aside from making him as comfortable as possible, there is little that can be done for him, according to the doctors. They tried to stall him off, but they finally decided to tell him the whole truth, which they

did day before yesterday. He is having good days and bad, ups and downs, as is to be expected, and must be given relief from pain with a succession of medicines. Dr. Wills says it is impossible to foretell how long he can last but that it might be a matter of weeks or even months.

Mrs. Fleischmann is bearing up wonderfully well, and my admiration for her grows and grows.

When I was director of the fish and game commission, I had made several motion pictures for the agency, and that fall the commission asked me to film a chukar hunt. With Judge Harold Taber and Harold Curran and their two Labrador retrievers, we made several hunts which I thought the Major might find interesting. So, omitting any mention of his illness, I wrote him. Shortly afterwards we received a handwritten letter from Mrs. Fleischmann:

Nevada and Buck my dears—

Just a line—as the Major is weak—very weak now. He is putting up a marvelous fight against insurmountable odds—Bless him. But he cannot eat—as hard as he tries—so his strength is going.

Nurses are very good. [The Major had been moved home.] You will know how I am feeling. But must keep up. Thank God my nights are quite good. You know my sister is here. Have not told him about Morley*—better not now.

Our days on the Haida were sad, but full of hope and I loved having both of you with me.

Your long letter to the Major, Buck, I read to him and he enjoyed it. Hard for him to concentrate for very long. All we can do is try to keep him comfortable as possible.

If you see Arthur Allen, Wingfields, or any other of the Major's friends please tell them all their messages have been appreciated.

No more now—Much love—

S. H. F.

*The Major's close friend, Morley Griswold, had died of a heart attack earlier that month.

Knowing the Major, I am certain that the worry and sadness his illness was causing Mrs. Fleischmann was of more concern to him than the pain he suffered. About eleven o'clock at night on October 16, 1951, Julius Bergen telephoned to tell us that the Major had died.[4]

Shortly after the Major's death, the quarterly bulletin of Santa Barbara's Museum of Natural History carried an article written by its president, Fred H. Schauer. The final paragraph of the article read:

> Major Fleischmann's interest and activity in this Museum was illustrative of his many-sided life. As business man, soldier, explorer, hunter, sportsman, traveller, scientist, philanthropist, and student of economics, he distinguished himself by always doing his utmost. He was a great example of the best of American manhood. And we believe that he was great as an American because he was a great Naturalist.

As I end this story, I think of the Sheep Bridge riffles, a thunderstorm over Kit Carson's pass, the desert bighorn on the Colorado, the beauty of our secret lake.

Those were good days, Major.

CHAPTER FIVE

His Legacy
(1951 – 1980)

Memorial services for Major Fleischmann were held in Santa Barbara, and several days later Lester Summerfield, the Major's Nevada attorney, called to request that I come to his office. An hour later I sat in front of his desk and listened to an incredible statement.

The Major and I had never discussed financial matters, and I had no knowledge of the trust agreement he had established early in 1951 between himself, as grantor, and Sarah Fleischmann, Julius Bergen, and Lester Summerfield as trustees. This agreement had been supplemented and implemented by his will to establish the Max C. Fleischmann Foundation of which I was one of the six trustees. In addition to the three original trustees and me, the foundation would be administered by two of the Major's long-time friends, Hugo A. Oswald of the Fleischmann Company and prominent New York attorney Walter G. Dunnington.

To say the least, I was amazed.

The will also requested that the trustees consider attorney Francis R. Breen of Reno to fill the first vacancy resulting from a death or resignation. Fran, an enthusiastic outdoor sportsman, had worked during the summers of his college and law school years on the Fleischmann's Glenbrook property and had fished with the Major.

Later that day I had an opportunity to study the trust agreement and learned that the trustees had been given broad powers regarding their methods of operation but that there were certain restrictions. Complete distribution of the trust's assets and termination of the trust must be made within twenty years after the death of Mrs. Fleischmann, and all grants were limited to projects within the United States. Funds could not be provided to any organization unless it was "organized and operated exclusively for religious, educational, charitable or scientific purposes, no part of the net earnings of which inures to the benefit of any private shareholder or individual, and no substantial part of the activities of which is carrying on propaganda, or otherwise attempting, to influence legislation."

Later, I learned that being a testamentary trust, the foundation would be supervised in its operation by the court in which the trust was established; and to this court the trustees would make an annual, detailed, audited report of all receipts, grants, and other expenditures. As a private foundation, the trust would also be regulated and audited by the Internal Revenue Service.

The Max C. Fleischmann Foundation was legally established on July 28, 1952, by decree of the First Judicial District Court of the State of Nevada, and shortly afterwards the board of trustees held its first formal meeting.

The five other trustees were highly qualified for the foundation's responsibilities. In addition to her general capableness and wisdom, Mrs. Fleischmann provided the board with intimate knowledge of the Major's past philanthropic interests.

As a young man, Julius Bergen had begun working for the Fleischmann Company at its offices in Chicago, eventually moving to the company's main office in New York where he became executive secretary to Julius Fleischmann, Chairman of the Board of Directors. When Max Fleischmann became chairman in 1925, Mr. Bergen became his executive secretary and moved to Santa Barbara, and on the Major's retirement in 1935, he persuaded Julius Bergen to leave the company and stay with him as his personal executive secretary. After twenty-five years of participation in Major Fleischmann's personal business affairs, Bergen's knowledge was invaluable to the foundation. In 1956 he received an honorary LL.D. degree from the University of Nevada.

Lester Summerfield, Major Fleischmann's Nevada attorney, was one of the most respected lawyers in the state. A

Five trustees of the Max C. Fleischmann Foundation at the dedication of the Fleischmann College of Agriculture building at the University of Nevada. Front row from left: Julius Bergen, Mrs. Sarah Fleischmann, Lester Summerfield, Walter Dunnington, and Sessions Wheeler. The sixth trustee, Hugo Oswald, was unable to attend.

native Nevadan, he had served as district attorney of Washoe County. Later the law firm of Summerfield and Heward became widely known in many other parts of the nation.

Walter G. Dunnington, Sr., a distinguished New York attorney and senior partner in the law firm of Dunnington, Bartholow and Miller, was a director of several large corporations including Standard Brands and the Colgate-Palmolive Co.; he had also been a former director of the Texas Company. He served as a trustee of the Seth Sprague Foundation and the Hanover Bank. An officer during World War I, he was wounded and, like the Major, gassed. For bravery in battle, Dunnington was awarded the Distinguished Service Cross. (His son, Walter G. Dunnington, Jr., is currently executive vice president and general counsel of Nabisco Brands, Inc.)

Hugo Oswald, a long-time and trusted friend of the Major, was treasurer of The Fleischmann Company and later of

Standard Brands. He was about the same age as Major Fleischmann and was able to serve only seven years on the foundation board, dying in 1959.

I was a good many years younger than the other members of the board and certainly less experienced in the world of business, finance, and law. I remember that during the morning of the first day of our two-day meeting, my contributions were limited to an occasional "second the motion."

During the afternoon, while something with which I was familiar was being discussed, I offered a suggestion which, I sensed, surprised several of the men at the table. One trustee opposed my proposal, while the others seemed undecided. Finally Lester Summerfield, chairman of the board, said, "Let's sleep on it and make a decision tomorrow." It was a mediation method he used successfully during future years, and it often resulted in a unanimous agreement.

But throughout the twenty-eight years of the foundation's lifetime, our decisions were not always unanimous—which was as it should have been. In this connection, I distinctly remember the aftermath of one incident.

Lester Summerfield was a formidably brilliant man; acquaintances would think twice or more before opposing him. I do not remember the issue, but it was a proposal which I definitely believed to be unwise, and I took him on in a rather heated argument. I do not recall the outcome, but at the conclusion of the meeting he remained sitting at the end of the conference table, and as I started to leave, he raised his hand to stop me. He smiled and said, "Buck, we had a good argument today, and you know something—I believe that if the Major was watching, he was smiling his approval."

Most of the larger foundations in the United States were operated by a professional staff with the trustees meeting only occasionally to establish general policies and consider staff recommendations. Our trust agreement would have allowed this type of procedure, but knowing the Major's preference, it was decided that the Fleischmann Foundation would be operated entirely by its trustees with only secretarial aid. It was believed that the combined background, experience, and training of the trustees in such fields as law, investment, accounting, education, science, conservation, etc., provided a variety of technical knowledge to aid them in their work; and the advice of specialized authorities could be sought as often as necessary.

We started operation in Lester's rather crowded law offices, with one full-time secretary. Until the Major's estate was settled, which required several years, the investment income available for granting was relatively small. Eventually we moved to larger offices with two, and finally three, secretaries. We shared the work—the chairman and two trustees managing the office. Investigating grant applications and preparing recommendations were the main responsibilities of the other three trustees. Mrs. Fleischmann participated actively by mail, telephone, and also in meetings during her Glenbrook months.

During most of the foundation's existence, daily conferences to discuss current requests were attended by the chairman and at least two other trustees. Every trustee received a copy of each request that met the foundation's requirements, and all letters were answered. Special meetings of the board were called whenever necessary, and regular meetings were held each month.

Following the death of Hugo Oswald in 1959, Francis Breen was elected a trustee, providing aid in legal affairs, investigations of grant requests, and other activities.

When Mrs. Sarah Fleischmann died in July of 1960, Thomas L. Little, manager of the Dean Witter brokerage firm office in Reno, was elected to the foundation's board of trustees. Shortly after his acceptance of the position, he retired from his former employment to devote full time to the foundation's investments and office responsibilities.

Lester D. Summerfield, chairman of the board of trustees, died in November of 1966. Julius Bergen was elected chairman, and Dr. Walter Orr Roberts of Boulder, Colorado, became a trustee. An internationally respected scientist, he provided extensive knowledge for the foundation's activities in scientific and educational fields.

In May of 1971, Walter G. Dunnington died. Because of the relatively few years remaining before the foundation's required termination, the court approved the board of trustees' opinion that the foundation should complete its responsibil-ities with its five experienced trustees. Julius Bergen continued to conscientiously chair the board for the final nine years of its existence.

Mention should be made of the capable secretaries who helped the office operate efficiently. We were fortunate in having the services of Mary Win Summerfield, Madeline Taylor, Clara Robison, Mary Date, and Mary Neff.

In some ways the twenty-eight years passed quickly; but looking back on the many thousands of requests, the difficult decisions, the multitude of grants, and the financial responsibilities, those years seem long ones. Many people, understandably, wished the foundation could have continued indefinitely, but Major Fleischmann's trust agreement was definite in requiring complete distribution of the trust twenty years after the death of his widow.

Assets received from the Major's estate totaled $63,864,452. Operating under a policy of conservative investment of the original assets, the foundation was able to grant $192,037,457 (income plus corpus). Over the twenty-eight years, organizations in Nevada received $89,155,251, or 46.4 percent of the total.

The trust agreement established the foundation as a national organization, and the trustees accepted that to be so. However, several factors, including the small number of major foundations located in the Far West during the 1950s and 1960s, affected the geographical distribution of Fleischmann funds. The trustees made an effort to support projects of national significance regardless of location.

Probably the fact that a relatively large foundation was operated by its trustees without a professional staff made the Fleischmann Foundation somewhat unique. In his book *The Big Foundations,* Waldemar A. Nielsen wrote that an experienced observer evaluated the Fleischmann Foundation in the following terms: "If I had to choose between professionalism and the Fleischmann kind of amateurism as a mode of Foundation operation, I would choose the latter. It is amateurism based on deep personal involvement and guided by great idealism and commitment."[1]

Regardless of whether the people who operated the Fleischmann Foundation were amateurs or professionals, they quietly attempted to respond to the Major's interests and accomplish what they believed were his goals. A recapitulation of the categories, numbers and amounts of grants made during twenty-eight years, follows:[2]

Category	Number of Grants	Total Granted
Education	413	$ 50,442,939.68
Medical Research	99	33,711,346.00
Medical Facilities	231	18,836,676.05
Youth	342	27,946,838.15
Conservation and Environment (including parks)	124	18,545,547.34
Non-medical Research	64	9,870,440.00
Libraries	55	8,061,838.42
Historical Preservation (museums, historical societies, historical structures)	69	8,884,385.73
Law	19	2,876,658.00
Religion	69	312,350.00
Health, Relief, Handicapped, and Community Projects	471	12,548,438.45
Total	1,956	$192,037,457.82

During his lifetime Major Fleischmann aided organizations in almost all of the above categories. In the following summaries, illustrations of grants in the various fields are largely limited to Nevada organizations.

Education

Many institutions of higher learning received Fleischmann support. Scholarship programs and other projects contributed to make education the foundation's largest field of activity.

During Max C. Fleischmann's lifetime, his gifts to the University of Nevada indicated his interest in the institution, and after 1952, the trustees followed his lead, making the university the largest single recipient of the foundation's funds.

Remembering a belief once expressed by Major Fleischmann that agricultural education was of vital importance to the state of Nevada, the trustees first provided funds to construct the Max C. Fleischmann College of Agriculture and the Sarah Hamilton Fleischmann School of Home Economics buildings. In following years nine additional building projects in which the foundation participated, in whole or part, included the Fleischmann Atmospherium-Planetarium, the Desert Research Institute's Center for Water Research, an environmental patho-physiology laboratory, the Judicial College building, College Inn purchase, Renewable Natural Resources and Life Sciences wings, and two medical school buildings.

Other grants covered scholarship programs, scientific equipment, books, and other necessities both in Nevada's two universities and in its community colleges. Over a period of twenty-eight years, foundation grants to the University of Nevada System, including the on-campus National Judicial College and the National Council of Juvenile and Family Court Judges, totaled more than $30 million.

In 1965, after extensive study of scholarship programs through-out the United States and guided by the concept that worthy students should be assisted to secure an education but not entirely relieved of the financial burdens which encourage responsibility and maturity, the foundation initiated a plan which educators have considered exceptionally successful.

The program was based on the belief that a student's freshman college year, during which he is adapting to a new environment and more demanding study habits, is the period during which financial or other aid is most beneficial, and that if he proves his ability that first year, non-interest loans, other scholarships, or part-time employment will become available. On that premise, 150 one-year, $1,000 scholarships were offered annually to the high schools of Nevada, apportioned according to their senior student enrollment, with a minimum of one scholarship to each school. So that each applicant's personal qualities and motivation could be considered by competent judges, the recipients were selected by individual school faculty committees. To allow student participation and provide maximum information, several student representatives were appointed as consultants to the committee.

Applicants were required to obtain a score in either the Scholastic Aptitude Test or the American College Test which indicated ability to do college work. Because students were competing for scholarships only against other students in the same school and under the same grading system, grades during the senior year were considered a valid selection criteria. Financial need was considered but was not a requisite for a scholarship.

Cooperating with the foundation, the Nevada State Department of Education administered the general scholarship program as well as others initiated in past years, such as four-year scholarships for Nevada medical and dental students, a scholarship program for Nevada Indian students, and the two experimental work-scholarship programs established in cooperation with the United States Forest Service and the Nevada State Fish and Game Commission, which allowed students to earn money for college while gaining experience in their fields of study.

Mrs. Wanda Biggs, who administered the Fleischmann scholarship programs for Nevada's department of education for over twenty-two years, wrote, "School administrators and teachers throughout Nevada have commended this program stating that the prestige and honor of receiving a Fleischmann scholarship have been major incentives for student study and achievement. . . . Most of the students awarded scholarships under the college program have received their bachelor's and have majored in a variety of fields. The effect of the scholarship program will never be fully evaluated or the derived benefits fully recognized."[3]

Grants in the field of education totaled over $50.4 million.

Medical Research

The field of medical research was the second largest recipient of foundation grants.

Probably partly influenced by Major Fleischmann's illness, support for the Sloan-Kettering Institute for Cancer Research began during the foundation's second year of operation (1953) and was continued periodically to total eventually more than $3 million. Throughout the years, support was provided to many other medical laboratories to aid in science's attempt to understand and control man's diseases. Seven grants to Stanford University Medical Center totaled over $7,600,000.

Whenever necessary the trustees sought advice from recognized authorities, and such aid was especially valuable in the field of medical research.

Medical research grants totaled approximately $33.7 million.

Medical Facilities

The long stretches of desert country separating most Nevada towns and an insufficiency of medical facilities and personnel in some rural communities became a matter of concern to the Fleischmann trustees early in the foundation's existence.

In 1959 the trustees requested the cooperation of the Nevada State Division of Health, Section of Medical Facilities, to conduct a statewide survey to determine the most urgent needs of the various hospitals. The survey resulted in grants to replace outmoded equipment, repairs to buildings, and funds to match federal grants for construction. Additional grants during the following years helped the hospitals to maintain modern equipment.

Because accidents on Nevada's highways, remote ranches, and mining camps often occur long distances from the nearest medical doctor, a state program, supported by federal and state funds, was initiated in 1975 to train rural volunteers as emergency medical technicians (EMTs). The foundation was able to help in this project by providing ambulances, rescue vehicles, and a specially equipped van for training EMTs. By 1979, the state had certified 3,372 technicians.

The next large step in providing emergency care to Nevadans began in 1977 with a grant to the Nevada Emergency Medical Services to develop an E.M.S. Radio Communication System. The system would provide pre-hospital care of injured or ill persons by hospital emergency room physicians who would be able to advise the ambulance team, highway patrol, or other rescue-vehicle technicians with direction and control of the level of care before and during transport to a hospital.

In 1979 the foundation trustees again requested the Nevada Division of Health for cooperation in conducting a new survey of medical facilities throughout the state with the purpose of making equipment grants. As a result of the survey, additional grants to Nevada hospitals amounted to approximately $5 million.

During the foundation's existence, grants for the above Nevada medical projects totaled approximately $14 million. Other states received about $4.8 million.

Youth

Major Fleischmann believed that out-of-doors experiences were of benefit to young people, and in the late 1930s aided the Nevada Area Council of the Boy Scouts in developing a Sierra camp which was eventually named Camp Fleischmann.

The foundation's grants in the field of youth were made to organizations in twenty-four different states. Outdoor camps, clubhouses, swimming pools, and gymnasiums were among the broad and diverse range of projects supported.

One hundred and sixty-five separate grants went to Boys' Clubs, Boy Scouts, Girls' Clubs, Girl Scouts, Camp Fire Girls, YMCAs, YWCAs, and other services aiding young people.

Within Nevada, grants to the above organizations and projects totaled more than $11.7 million. Nationwide, grants in this field totaled approximately $28 million.

Conservation and Environment

Major Fleischmann's enjoyment of natural environments was well known, and his foundation's environmental and conservation grants have covered a wide variety of both large and small projects in fields of land acquisition, protection of watersheds, pollution control, wildlife and fisheries studies, waterfowl marsh restoration, rural and urban parklands, and others.

In 1970 concern for Lake Tahoe's environment created a cooperative project with the state of Nevada for purchase of land on the east side of the lake. The foundation's grant of $1.5 million, combined with the state legislature's appropriation and federal funds, brought state ownership of land in the basin to over 13,000 acres.

Another Lake Tahoe conservation project in the 1960s was concerned primarily with water pollution. Under a foundation award to the Lake Tahoe Area Council, a team of consultants composed of the world's foremost authorities and a leading sanitary engineering firm, developed a plan for disposal of the sewage in the Tahoe basin.

Ducks Unlimited's waterfowl-breeding marsh restoration was one of Major Fleischmann's special interests. As a trustee of Ducks Unlimited in the United States and a director of its Canadian branch for many years, he was widely known for his work and support of the organization, and his foundation continued to provide financial aid to this large conservation movement.

The Nevada State Department of Fish and Game received grants for fisheries studies in Pyramid, Walker, and Tahoe lakes and for waterfowl areas, bighorn sheep restoration, and other projects.

Grants in the field of conservation and environment totaled approximately $18.5 million.

Non-Medical Research

In the field of non-medical research, foundation grants funded a wide range of projects which included support of studies of the earth's atmosphere, its deserts, and its oceans.

Grants to the University of Nevada's Desert Research Institute began in 1960, and during the following years made funds available for a building for its Center for Water Resources Research, for equipment, and for various projects including atmospheric studies.

Grants for non-medical research totaled approximately $9.9 million.

Libraries

In the 1960s, recognizing a particular need for the development of library resources in Nevada and believing that a library can be an important cultural center of a community (offering both educational and recreational values), the foundation began providing grants which eventually helped construct eighteen libraries throughout Nevada.

Nevada library grants totaled approximately $8 million.

Historical Preservation

During his lifetime Major Fleischmann had a special interest in and provided substantial support to two museums, the Nevada State Museum and the Santa Barbara Museum of Natural History.

From its beginning, the foundation periodically aided the Nevada State Museum, providing a total of approximately $3 million during the twenty-eight years. The Santa Barbara Museum of Natural History received $1,400,000, the Northeastern Nevada Museum was granted $950,000, and sixteen other Nevada historical preservation organizations received foundation aid. Total grants in this field amounted to $8.8 million.

Law

Considered a project of exceptional importance to the entire country, the National Judicial College (with headquarters on the University of Nevada, Reno campus) was the recipient of more than $8 million in Fleischmann grants over a period of fourteen years. These grants were included in the university's total.

The foundation also awarded six grants totaling almost $2 million to the University of the Pacific's McGeorge School of Law where many Nevada law students receive their training. The grant total in this field, not including the National Judicial College, was approximately $2.9 million.

Religion

During the foundation's early years, several churches in small Nevada communities were given construction and repair aid, totaling about $312,000.

Health, Relief, Handicapped, and Community Projects

Approximately $12.5 million were granted to organizations concerned with either health, relief, or social projects.

The American Red Cross received special grants for emergency situations. Other types of projects included those concerned with the blind, mentally retarded, physical rehabilitation, alcohol and drug abuse, senior citizens, and economically and socially deprived children.

A foundation grant to the Martinez, California, Early Childhood Center resulted in several thank-you letters from pre-school youngsters there. One of the carefully written notes included a postscript which brought a smile:

Dear Mr. Fleischmann—
I would really like to thank you.
If it wasnt for Max C. Fleischmann
foundation we wouldn't even exist.
Thank you.

from Tim
P.S. Nice going Max!

146

Notes

Chapter 2. Origins, Business, and the Adventure Years

1. William Coyle, *Ohio Authors and Their Books . . . 1796–1950* (Cleveland: World Publishing Co., 1962), pp. 214–15.
2. "Fleischmann from Hungary," chapter 15 of *They Helped Make America*, pp. 189–97. This undated manuscript was found among the Major's papers.
3. Ibid.
4. Ibid.; Julius Bergen, interviews with author in 1983 and 1984.
5. Ibid.
6. Ibid.
7. Julius Bergen, interviews with author.
8. "Fleischmann from Hungary."
9. Julius Bergen, interviews with author.
10. National Archives, Military Service Branch, Military Archives Division (Washington, D.C.), Record Group 94.
11. Ibid.
12. *Who Was Who in America*, vol. 3 (Chicago: The A.N. Marquis Company, 1960), p. 287.
13. Max C. Fleischmann, *After Big Game in Arctic and Tropic* (Cincinnati: The Jennings and Graham Press, 1909).
14. John Edwards Caswell, *Arctic Frontiers: United States Explorations in the Far North* (Norman: University of Oklahoma Press, 1956), pp. 170–71. Between 1894 and 1909, Walter Wellman, a president of the National Press Club of Washington, D.C., made six unsuccessful attempts to reach the North Pole. The first two were by dog sledge, the other four by motor-powered balloon airships. On the expedition in 1906, motor failures and an unstable "airship hall" ended the expedition at Danes Island.
15. Ibid., p. 166. In 1897, Salomon August Andrée of Sweden attempted to reach the North Pole in a balloon. He failed and died of carbon monoxide poisoning while within his tent.
16. Cincinnati *Times-Star*, September 16, 1909. (First published in the London *Times* in 1907.)
17. Charles F. Goss, ed., *Cincinnati, the Queen City, 1788–1912*, vol. 4 (Chicago and Cincinnati: The S. J. Clarke Publishing Co., 1912), pp. 199–200.

18. Max C. Fleischmann, letter of application for commission in the Signal Officers' Reserve Corps, March 28, 1917, National Archives, Military Archives Division (Washington, D.C.), Record Group 94; [Julius Bergen?], material prepared for cornerstone-laying of Fleischmann College of Agriculture, University of Nevada, June 14, 1957.

19. National Archives, Military Service Branch, Military Archives Division (Washington, D.C.), Record Group 94.

20. Ibid., Record Group 120.

21. Santa Barbara *News-Press,* October 17, 1951.

22. Santa Barbara Museum of History, *Museum Talk* (Fall 1951): pp. 25–29.

23. Santa Barbara Museum of History, *Museum Talk* (Winter 1950–51): pp. 51–52.

24. John H. Wells, *America's Outstanding Seagoing Diesel Yacht, Haida* (New York), 12-page promotional brochure.

Chapter 3. The Nevada Years

1. James L. Clark, "Fleischmann-Clark, American Museum, Indo-China Expedition," *Natural History,* vol. 38 (December 1936), pp. 385–90.

2. *New York Times,* June 9, 1936.

3. *Who Was Who in America,* vol. 3, p. 287.

4. Clark J. Guild, *Memories of My Work as a Lyon County Official, Nevada District Judge, and Nevada State Museum Founder,* (Reno: Oral History Program, University of Nevada, 1967), pp. 213–25; idem, "Start of the Museum Mine," Judge Guild Collection, Nevada State Museum, Carson City.

5. Guy Shipler, "Max and His Millions," *Nevada* (July–August 1980), pp. 11–13.

6. Max C. Fleischmann, letter to author, November 3, 1944.

7. Santa Barbara *News-Press,* April 17, 1956.

8. *Reno Evening Gazette,* July 2, 1947.

Chapter 4. The Last Years

1. Jimmy Robinson, "Max Fleischmann . . . a Sportsman for All Time," *The American Shotgunner* (March 1982), pp. 26–29. This article was made available through the cooperation of Mr. Robinson and the magazine's publisher, Bob Thruston.

2. Jimmy Robinson, *The Best of Jimmy Robinson* (Detroit Lakes, Minnesota: John R. Meyer, 1980), p. 42.

3. John H. Wells, *America's Outstanding Seagoing Diesel Yacht, Haida.*

4. The Major kept a revolver near his bed. Not knowing how long his hopeless condition would last, the Major shot himself, I am certain, to spare Mrs. Fleischmann any further anguish.

Chapter 5. His Legacy

1. Waldemar A. Nielsen, *The Big Foundations*, A Twentieth Century Fund Study (New York: Columbia University Press, 1972), p. 254.
2. Sessions S. Wheeler, comp., *Max C. Fleischmann Foundation, Twenty-Eight Years: A Narrative Report of the Foundation's Activities, from July 28, 1952 to June 30, 1980* (Reno, 1980).
3. Ibid.

Index